W9-CIX-220

can't
find

LEWIS MUMFORD

Sticks and Stones

A Study of American
Architecture and Civilization

DOVER PUBLICATIONS, INC., NEW YORK

*Architecture, properly understood,
is civilization itself.*

W. R. LETHABY

*What is civilization? It is the humani-
zation of man in society.*

MATTHEW ARNOLD

COPYRIGHT 1924 BY
BONI AND LIVERIGHT, INC.

SECOND REVISED EDITION
COPYRIGHT © 1955 BY
DOVER PUBLICATIONS, INC.

*All rights reserved under Pan American and
international copyright conventions.*

Library of Congress Catalog Card Number: 58-14337

Manufactured in the United States of America

Dover Publications, Inc.
180 Varick Street
New York 14, N.Y.

PREFACE: 1954

THIS book was published just thirty years ago. In bringing it forth in a new edition, it will be useful, perhaps, if I indicate not only the changes I have made in the text, but also if I likewise explain my reluctance to make more generous emendations. At the same time, I shall seize the moment to give the reader who comes to *Sticks and Stones* without any other background some acquaintance with my present views.

When this book was first published, in 1924, no history of American architecture as a whole had yet been written: even Fiske Kimball's and Thomas Tallmadge's modest essays had still to appear. While a new generation of literary critics, headed by Mr. Van Wyck Brooks, was awakening American interest in the unsuspected richness of our literary past, no equivalent movement was yet visible in architecture. The post-colonial expanse of American architecture was virgin territory: that land beckoned to the pathfinder, the prospector, the pioneer. *In Sticks and Stones*, the first rapid exploration was made.

Such a book could have been written only by a young man, with no reputation to risk, with no vested interest to protect, bold to the point of recklessness, and ready to intrude where professors, if not angels, would fear to tread. Doubtless if I had had a better sense of the difficulties or of my own limitations, I should have left the field alone.

For the reader to understand what was involved in this first exploration, I must remind him of the state of American architectural research at that point. Following the colonial revival, which began in the seventies, a considerable amount of detailed study had been done on the early architecture of the North Atlantic States and Virginia: local historians had hardly even begun the systematic investigation of other parts of the country. Fiske Kimball's magistral study of the *Domestic Architecture of the Colonies and the Early Republic* was the consummation of these early studies. But even for New England, the story of American architecture after 1850 was a pathless waste. By 1924, the work of the Chicago school, historically speaking, had dropped out of sight completely. This means that for the historian the most creative period in American architecture, that between 1880 and 1900, did not yet exist.

All that an interpretation of "American architecture and civilization" could hope to accomplish under these circumstances was to make a swift, necessarily superficial sampling of these hidden veins and lodes and bring back a few geologist's fragments. For this purpose my training had perhaps prepared me better than that of most of my contemporaries; for, as a practicer of civic and regional surveying, I had explored with a notebook and camera the cities and villages of the Eastern seaboard; and had learned to use buildings as documents, in much the same fashion that the archaeologist does. Fortunately, my insight into the processes of building was constantly sharpened by association with the remarkable group of architects, engineers, planners, and "geotects"—as our beloved Benton MacKaye likes to call himself— who in 1923 formed the Regional Planning Association of America.

Given the state of the subject, *Sticks and Stones* turned out to be a more adequate sketch than my most sanguine friends could have hoped. In a moment, I shall deal with some of its inadequacies, its misinterpretations, its omissions; but first, if the reader will forgive the immodesty, let me call attention to its positive contributions. To begin with, it was one of the first books to do justice to the medieval traditions in America: for I showed that the early towns did not belong to the New World, but were transpositions of the forms and institutions of the late medieval towns and villages in Europe. With this went possibly the first written appreciation of the New England village as an architectural entity. Here, and in the chapter on the Renaissance, I stressed the importance of vernacular building, usually overlooked by historians, whose interest in a building was often in proportion to the extent it imitated correctly the more genteel models of the Old World. My chief contribution to an appraisal of the architecture of the Colonial and Federal periods was to demonstrate that it was organically part of the culture of the time; hence, it could not be fitted into our own radically different scheme of life. This point of view is now commonplace; yet a generation ago it was still rare.

But in the period after the Civil War, *Sticks and Stones* made its shrewdest contributions; and first of all, by restoring to their proper position, the work and example of Henry Hobson Richardson: our first truly indigenous master-builder. Richardson's heyday had

been in the eighties, when he dominated the scene.
The last reference of importance to Richardson was
Montgomery Schuyler's estimate in *American Architecture*, 1893. For a generation Richardson's work,
so far as it was not entirely forgotten, had become
a butt and a jest, a byword for all that was stuffy
and outmoded. My chapter on his work struck the
first blow against this glib, fashionable judgment and
led the way toward his rehabilitation. But even I, in
1924, had not yet appreciated the truly original qualities in Richardson's last work; so I repeated the old
mistake of characterizing him as a mere romanticist.

At the same time, I had the honor to lead the way
in another renewal of architectural values: an understanding of the genius of John A. Roebling and his
son, Washington, the builders of the Brooklyn Bridge.
This again was the first fresh criticism of their work
after Montgomery Schuyler's superb analysis, which
I recently republished in *The Roots of Contemporary
American Architecture*. At the same time I was writing about the Bridge, the poet, Hart Crane, living a
few blocks from me on Brooklyn Heights, was composing his poem on the same theme. Our common appreciation of this great work of art became part of
a wider movement, which owes so much to the polariz-

ing effect of *The Seven Arts* and *The New Republic*: the working toward the creation of a "usable past" for our country.

After that chapter, *Sticks and Stones* exposes a real hiatus, due simply to my ignorance. The interpretation jumped from Richardson and Roebling into the Imperial and Classical revival, which started with the World's Fair of 1893, without doing even faint justice to the great architectural innovations, both in content and form, that one now associates with the work of the Chicago school: in particular with that of Burnham and Root, Adler and Sullivan, Holabird and Roche, and Major Le Baron Jenney. These great pioneers of New World architecture formed a bridge between Richardson, with his Marshall Field Warehouse, in Chicago, and Louis Sullivan's continuator, Frank Lloyd Wright, who, in the free flight of constructive imagination, soars above all his contemporaries.

Here, plainly, the prime virtue of *Sticks and Stones*, that it rested on first-hand observations and first-hand judgments, became a defect: I omitted any but passing references to Sullivan and Wright because I had not yet visited Chicago and had not yet seen their work. When finally I spent three weeks in Chicago in 1927 and toured the Loop with Barry Byrne, whose work linked Wright's prairie period and the twenties, I discovered with delight the great office-buildings and warehouses of that early period: buildings of classic simplicity of form, whose sober excellence had been spurned by the copybook classicists and cakefrosting eclectics of the next generation. My first appreciation of work, in the pages of *Architecture* in 1928, was again far from adequate; but apart from the contributions of European visitors, like Walter Curt Behrendt and Eric Mendelsohn, it had the merit of being perhaps the first to single out the significance of other innovators besides Sullivan and Wright. This omission was painful, once I noted it; but to interpolate a new chapter in *Sticks and Stones* without re-writing the whole book would have been impossible: hence my first studied attempt to correct the lopsided picture I had given there came only in 1931, when I wrote *The Brown Decades*.

A warning word about the chapter on The Age of the Machine: an appraisal sometimes just in negative criticism, but weak in positive insight. My first approach to the machine, in a little essay called Machinery and the Modern Style which came out in 1921, was an affirmative one; and my original plan called for a chapter on The New Vernacular of the Machine. But in the spring of 1923, meeting Patrick Geddes in New York for the first time, I fell under the spell of his sharp critical reaction against our machine-ridden civilization; and when I came to write this chapter shortly after, I had not yet arrived at the balanced judgment I sought to achieve, in 1934, in *Technics and Civilization*. I shall not bother to disentangle what is sound from what is erratic in this chapter, for *The Brown Decades* provides much of the corrective knowledge necessary. But I would point out that my most challenging judgment—the social criticism of the skyscraper as a promoter of urban congestion and disorder, when not under severe social discipline—still holds: in fact, time has only piled up further confirmation.

I have left to the last perhaps the greatest contribution that *Sticks and Stones* made, though it is one that has not yet, I regret to say, been fully absorbed by critics and historians of architecture. This is the fact that I sought to relate individual structures to their urban site or their setting in the rural landscape: thus I turned my back upon the habit of treating the building as a self-sufficient entity, an esthetic abstraction; and in doing this, I not merely did justice to social conditions but also gave due esthetic importance to the whole mass of building that necessarily serves as background for the outstanding works of civic and religious architecture. The single building is but an element in a complex civic or landscape design. Except in the abstraction of drawing or photography no building exists in a void: it functions as part of a greater whole and can be seen and felt only through dynamic participation in that whole. This seems to me a fundamental doctrine; but it has yet to be widely honored. Dr. Walter Curt Behrendt's *Modern Building* was perhaps the first work after *Sticks and Stones* to give due recognition to this social-esthetic relationship.

If *Sticks and Stones* is still readable, it is in spite of the serious omissions and misinterpretations to which I have called the reader's attention. More than once, during the last twenty years, I have been tempted to revise the book radically; but however imperative the corrections of detail, such a revision would ruin the one quality *Sticks and Stones* still possesses: its unity as a work of art. For this reason I have even avoided the temptation to remove callow judgments, like my echo of Ruskin's criticism of the Crystal Palace or my attempt to find extraordinary

virtues in one of Helmle and Corbett's early loft buildings, before I had become acquainted with the Chicago
school. Nevertheless, in order to leave a few signposts
for the otherwise unsuspecting lay reader, I have
taken the present opportunity to add a final para-
graph to each of Chapters One to Five, and again
to Chapter Seven, even at some risk of contradiction.
In addition, I have corrected the few factual errors
that have come to light.

The moment for writing such a book as *Sticks and
Stones* is now past. Before it can come again, by way
of a definitive summary, we must absorb the vast
amount of material that has emerged during the last
thirty years: material that is only now being put
together in such monumental surveys as that which
Professor Hugh Morrison has begun. Even then, there
is still a whole series of further investigations to be
made not only on the whole span of industrial and
domestic building after 1850, but also on the planning
and layout of villages, neighborhoods and cities, along
the lines followed with such admirable thoroughness
by Professor Anthony Garvan, in his study of Connecticut towns. From the standpoint of American
architectural history *Sticks and Stones* has perforce
become just another document. If I have any abiding

Preface: 1954

satisfaction over this work of my youth, it is in the pioneer's secret pride that scholarly buildings are now being built, in distant historic territory, over the buried ashes of a hasty campfire I once lighted, near a spring from whose waters I was the first explorer to drink.

LEWIS MUMFORD

CONTENTS

PLATES

Opposite
page

Sticks and Stones

The illustrations for this edition have been selected by Adolf Placzek, Columbia University.

CHAPTER ONE

THE MEDIEVAL TRADITION

For a hundred years or so after its settlement, there lived and flourished in America a type of community which was rapidly disappearing in Europe. This community was embodied in villages and towns whose mummified remains even today have a rooted dignity that the most gigantic metropolises do not often possess. If we would understand the architecture of America in a period when good building was almost universal, we must understand something of the kind of life that this community fostered.

The capital example of the medieval tradition lies in the New England village.

There are two or three things that stand in the way of our seeing the life of a New England village; and one of them is the myth of the pioneer, the conception of the first settlers as a free band of "Americans" throwing off the bedraggled garments of Europe and starting life afresh in the wilderness. So far from giving birth to a new life, the settlement of the northern American seaboard prolonged for a little while the social habits and economic institutions which were fast crumbling away in Europe, particularly in England. In the villages of the New World there flickered up the last dying embers of the medieval order.

Whereas in England the common lands were being confiscated for the benefit of an aristocracy, and the arable turned into sheep-runs for the profit of the great proprietors, in New England the common lands were re-established with the founding of a new settlement. In England the depauperate peasants and yeomen were driven into the large towns to become the casual workers, menials, and soldiers; in New England, on the other hand, it was at first only with threats of punishment and conscription that the town workers were kept from going out into the countryside to seek a more independent living from the soil. Just as the archaic speech of the Elizabethans has lingered in the Kentucky Mountains, so the Middle Ages at their best lingered along the coast of Appalachia; and in the organization of our New England villages one sees a greater resemblance to the medieval Utopia of Sir Thomas More than to the classic republic in the style of Montesquieu, which was actually founded in the eighteenth century.

The colonists who sought to establish permanent communities—as distinct from those who erected only trading posts—were not a little like those whom the cities of Greece used to plant about the Mediterranean and the Black Sea littoral. Like the founders of the "Ancient City," the Puritans first concerned themselves to erect an altar, or rather, to lay the foundations for an edifice which denied the religious value of altars. In the crudest of "smoaky wigwams," an early observer notes, the Puritans remember to "sing psalms, pray, and praise their God"; and although we of today may regard their religion as harsh and nay-saying, we cannot forget that it was a central point of their existence and not an afterthought piled as it were on material prosperity for the sake of a good appearance. Material goods formed the basis, but not the end, of their life.

The meeting-house determined the character and limits of the community. As Weeden says in his excellent Economic and Social History of New England, the settlers "laid out the village in the best order to attain two objects: first, the tillage and culture of the soil; second, the maintenance of a 'civil and religious society.'" Around the meeting-house the rest of the community crystallized in a definite pattern, tight and homogeneous.

The early provincial village bears another resemblance to the early Greek city: it does not continue to grow at such a pace that it either becomes overcrowded within or spills beyond its limits into dejected suburbs; still less does it seek what we ironically call greatness by increasing the number of its inhabitants. When the corporation has a sufficient number of members, that is to say, when the land is fairly occupied, and when the addition of more land would unduly increase the hardship of working it from the town, or would spread out the farmers, and make it difficult for them to attend to their religious and civil duties, the original settlement throws out a new shoot. So Charlestown threw off Woburn; so Dedham colonized Medfield; so Lynn founded Nahant.

The Puritans knew and applied a principle that Plato had long ago pointed out in The Republic, namely, that an intelligent and socialized community will continue to grow only as long as it can remain a unit and keep up its common institutions. Beyond that point growth must cease, or the community will disintegrate and cease to be an organic thing. Economically, this method of community-development kept land values at a properly low level, and prevented the engrossing of land for the sake of a speculative rise. The advantage of the Puritan method of settlement comes out plainly when one contrasts it with the trader's paradise of Manhattan; for by the middle of the seventeenth century all the land on Manhattan Island was privately owned, although only a small part of it was cultivated, and so eagerly had the teeth of monopoly bitten into this fine morsel that there was already a housing-shortage.

One more point of resemblance: all the inhabitants of an early New England village were co-partners in a corporation; they admitted into the community only as many members as they could assimilate. This co-partnership was based upon a common sense as to the purpose of the community, and upon a roughly equal divison of the land into individual plots taken in freehold, and a share of the common fields, of which there might be half a dozen or more.

There are various local differences in the apportionment of the land. In many cases, the minister and deacons have a larger share than the rest of the community; but in Charlestown, for example, the poorest had six or seven acres of meadow and twenty-five or thereabouts of upland; and this would hold pretty well throughout the settlements. Not merely is membership in the community guarded: the right of occupying and transferring the land is also restricted, and again and again, in the face of the General Assembly, the little villages make provisions to keep the land from changing hands without the consent of the corporation; "it being our real intent," as the burghers of Watertown put it, to "sitt down there close togither."

These regulations have a positive side as well; for in some cases the towns helped the poorer members of the corporation to build houses, and as a new member was voted into the community, lots were assigned immediately, without further ado. A friend of mine has called this system "Yankee communism," and I cheerfully bring the institution to the attention of those who do not realize upon what subversive principles Americanism, historically, rests.

What is true of the seventeenth century in New England holds good for the eighteenth century in the

Moravian settlements of Pennsylvania; and it is doubtless true for many another obscure colony; for the same spirit lingered, with a parallel result in architecture and industry, in the utopian communities of the nineteenth century. It is pretty plain that this type of pioneering, this definite search for the good life, was conducted on an altogether different level from the ruthless exploitation of the individual muckers and scavengers who hit the trail west of the Alleghanies. Such renewals of the earlier European culture as the Bach Festival at Bethlehem give us a notion of the cultural values which the medieval community carried over from the Old World to the New. There is some of this spirit left even in the architecture of the Shaker community at Mount Lebanon, New York, which was built as late as the nineteenth century.

In contrast to the New England village-community was the trading post. Of this nature were the little towns in the New Netherlands which were planted there by the Dutch West India Company: the settlers were for the most part either harassed individuals who were lured to the New World by the prospects of a good living, or people of established rank who were tempted to leave the walks of commerce for the dignities and affluences that were attached to the feudal tenure of the large estates that lined the Hudson.

The germs of town life came over with these people, and sheer necessity turned part of their energies to agriculture, but they did not develop the close village-community we find in New England; and though New Amsterdam was a replica of the Old World port, with its gabled brick houses, and its well-banked canals and fine gardens, it left no decided pattern on the American scene. It is only the country architecture of the Dutch which survives as either a relic or a memory. These trading posts like Manhattan and Fort Orange were, as Messrs. Petersen and Edwards have shown in their study of New York as an Eighteenth Century Municipality, medieval in their economy: numerous guild and civic regulations which provided for honest weight and measure and workmanship continued in force within the town. In their external dealings, on the other hand, the practice of the traders was sharp, and every man was for himself. Beginning its life by bargaining in necessities, the trading post ends by making a necessity of bargaining; and it was the impetus from its original commercial habits which

determined the characteristics of the abortive city
plan that was laid down for Manhattan Island in
1811. Rich as the Dutch precedent is in individual
farmhouses, it brings us no pattern, such as we
find in New England, for the community as a
whole.

II

Since we are accustomed to look upon the village as a quaint primitive relic of a bygone age, we
do not readily see that its form was dictated by social
and economic conditions. Where the village had to
defend itself against Indians, it was necessary to lay
it out completely, so that it might be surrounded by
a stockade, and so that the meeting-house might be
such a rallying center as the bell-tower or the castle
was in Europe, or as the high temple site was in
classic times. But in the eighteenth century the
Indian figured less in the scheme of colonial life,
and along the seacoast and river—as at Wells Beach
in Maine or Litchfield in Connecticut—the village
became a long strip upon a highroad, and the
arable land stretched in narrow plots from the house
to the water, so that the farmer might better
protect his crops and his livestock from the fox,

the wolf, the woodchuck, the hawk, the skunk, and the deer.

I emphasize these points of structure because of the silly notion superficial observers sometimes carry away from the villages of Europe or New England; namely, that their irregularity is altogether capricious and uneconomical, associated only with the vagaries of the straying cow. It would be more correct to say that the precise reverse was true. The inequality in size and shape of plots shows always that attention was paid to the function the land was to perform, rather than to the mere possession of property. Thus, there was a difference in size between home lots, which were always seated in the village, and purely agricultural tracts of land, which were usually on the outskirts; and in Dedham, for example, married men had home lots of twelve acres, while bachelors received only eight. Another reason for the compactness of the village was a decree of the General Court in Massachusetts, in 1635, that no dwelling should be placed more than half a mile from the meeting-house in any new plantation. Even irregularities in the layout and placement of houses, which cannot be referred to such obvious points as these, very often derive from an attempt to break the path of the wind, to get a good exposure in summer, or to profit by a view.

All this was genuine community planning. It did not go by this name, perhaps, but it achieved the result.

III

We have learned in recent years to appreciate the felicities of eighteenth-century colonial architecture, and even the earlier seventeenth-century style is now coming into its own, in the sense that it is being imitated by architects who have an eye for picturesque effects; but we lose our perspective altogether if we think that the charm of an old New England house can be recaptured by designing overhanging second stories or panelled interiors. The just design, the careful execution, the fine style that brings all the houses into harmony no matter how diverse the purposes they served—for the farmhouse shares its characteristics with the mill, and the mill with the meeting-house—was the outcome of a common spirit, nourished by men who had divided the land fairly and who shared adversity and good fortune together. When the frame of the house is to be raised, a man's neighbors will lend him a hand; if the harvest is in danger, every man goes out into the fields, even if his own crop is not at stake; if a whale founders on the beach, even the smallest boy bears a hand, and gets a share of the reward. All these practices were not without their subtle effect upon craftsmanship.

Schooled in the traditions of his guild, the medieval carpenter pours his all into the work. Since sale does not enter into the bargain, it is both to his patron's advantage to give him the best materials, and to his own advantage to make the most of them. If at first, in the haste of settlement, the colonists are content with makeshifts, they are nevertheless done in the traditional fashion—not the log cabins of later days, but, more probably, wattle and daub huts like those of the charcoal burners in the English forests. In some points, the prevailing English tradition does not fit the raw climate of the north, and presently the half-timbered houses of some of the earlier settlers would be covered by clapboards for greater warmth, as in the eighteenth century their interiors were lined with panelled pine or oak, instead of the rough plaster. No matter what the material or mode, the carpenter works not simply for hire, but for dear life's sake, and as a baker's dozen numbers thirteen, so a piece of handicraft contains not merely the workmanship itself, but a bit of the worker's soul, for good measure. The new invention of the gambrel roof, which gave additional room to the second story without raising the roof-tree, is a product of this system; and the variation in its length and pitch in New England, New Jersey, and New York is a witness to the freedom of design that prevailed throughout the work.

These seventeenth-century houses, built at first with one or two rooms, and then as luxury increased and family needs multiplied with as many as four, would doubtless seem unspeakably crude and mean to the resident of Floral Heights; indeed, if our present requirements for housing were so simple it would not be quite so difficult to meet our perpetual shortage. As a matter of fact, however, these early provincial houses were well up to the standards for a similar homestead in England; and in some ways were a distinct advance. Just as all the separate courses on a restaurant menu were a few hundred years ago cooked in the same pot, so the different subdivisions of the modern house were originally combined into a single room, which was not merely kitchen, workroom, and living quarters, but which also, at least in winter, served as a stable for the more delicate members of the barnyard. By the time America was settled the division into rooms had just commenced among the better sort of farmer: the barn had split off from the rest of the house, and the bedchamber was becoming a separate apartment. As the seventeenth century lengthened, this division of functions became more familiar in the provincial house.

Let us take a brief look at one of these seventeenth-century buildings; let us say, the John Ward house in Salem which still survives as a relic. As one approaches the village on some November day, when the leaves are no longer on the trees to obscure the vista, one feels the dynamic quality of medieval architecture—a quality altogether different from the prudent regularities of the later Georgian mode. It is not merely a matter of painted gables, leaded, diamond-paned windows, overhanging second stories, much as these would perhaps remind us of a medieval European town. What would attract one is the feeling, not of formal abstract design, but of growth: the house has developed as the family within it has

Courtesy Ware Library, Columbia University

PLATE ONE   *John Ward House. Salem, Mass. (1684)*

prospered, and brought forth children; as sons and daughters have married, as children have become more numerous, there have been additions: by a lean-to at one end the kitchen has achieved a separate existence, for instance; and these unpainted, weathered oaken masses pile up with a cumulative richness of effect.

Every step that brings one nearer to the house alters the relation of the planes formed by the gable ends; and so one must have got the same effect in these old village streets as one gets today when one skirts around, let us say, Notre Dame in Paris, now overwhelmed by the towers at the front, and now seeing them reduced to nothing by the tall spire in the rear. So the building seems in motion, as well as the spectator; and this quality delights the eye quite as much as formal decoration, which the architecture of the seventeenth century in America almost completely lacked.

The Puritan had his failings; and this lack of decoration was perhaps the most important one in architecture. In his devotion to books and in his love for music, even psalm-music, the Puritan was not immune to art; but he was suspicious of· the image, and one is tempted to read into his idol-breaking a positive visual defect, akin to the Daltonism or color blindness of the Quakers. Whereas medieval architecture had cherished the sculptor and the painter, even in the commonest vernacular work, the Puritans looked upon every diversion of the eye as a diversion from the Lord, and, by forbidding a respectable union between the artist and the useful arts, they finally turned the artist out on the streets, to pander to the first fine gentleman who would give him a kind word or a coin. Whereas Puritan buildings in the seventeenth century were straightforward and honestly bent to fulfill their functions, the Puritan did not see that ornament itself may be functional, too, when it expresses some positive gesture of the spirit. The bareness of the seventeenth century paved the way for the finicking graces of the eighteenth.

IV

In essentials, however, both the life and the architecture of the first provincial period are sound. While agriculture is the mainstay of life, and the medieval tradition flourishes, the New England village reaches a pretty fair pitch of worldly

perfection; and beneath all the superficial changes
that affected it in the next century and a half,
its sturdy framework held together remarkably
well.

Consider the village itself. In the center is a
common, a little to one side will be the meeting-
house, perhaps a square barnlike structure, with a
hipped roof and a cupola, like that at Hingham;
and adjacent or across the way will be the grammar
school. Along the roads where the houses are set
at regular intervals is a great columnar arcade of
elm trees. All these elements are essential to our
early provincial architecture, and without them it
would be a little bare and forbidding. The trees,
above all, are an important part of New England
architecture: in summer they absorb the moisture
and cool the air, besides giving shade; in the winter
their huge boles serve as a partial windbrake; even
the humus from their leaves keeps the soil of the
lawns in better order. The apple trees and kitchen-
garden, giving food and beauty, are not less essential. Would it be an exaggeration to say that there
has never been a more complete and intelligent part-
nership between the earth and man than existed, for
a little while, in the old New England village? In

what other part of the world has such a harmonious balance between the natural and the social environment been preserved?

Nowadays we have begun to talk about garden cities, and we realize that the essential elements in a garden-city are the common holding of land by the community, and the coöperative ownership and direction of the community itself. We refer to all these things as if they represented a distinct achievement of modern thought; but the fact of the matter is that the New England village up to the middle of the eighteenth century was a garden-city in every sense that we now apply to that term, and happily its gardens and its harmonious framework have frequently lingered on, even though the economic foundations have long been overthrown.

This is a medieval tradition in American architecture which should be of some use to our architects and city planners; for it is a much more substantial matter than the building of perpendicular churches or Tudor country-houses in painfully archæological adaptations. If we wish to tie up with our colonial tradition we must recover more than the architectural forms: we must recover the interests, the standards, the institutions that gave to the villages and

PLATE TWO   *Fairbanks House. Dedham, Mass.*

buildings of early times their appropriate shapes.
To do much less than this is merely to bring back
a fad which might as well be Egyptian as "colonial"
for all the sincerity that it exhibits.

Wherever these villages were well-established, they
kept sweet and sound over the centuries: in Connecticut, Sharon and Litchfield and Old Lyme; in Massachusetts, Shirley Center and Harvard and Andover;
Manchester in Vermont, or Thetford in New Hamp-
shire, still bear testimony to the life-wisdom and skill
of their early planners and inhabitants. This organic
form of village, so far from disappearing with the
nineteenth century, provided a model for the new
villages of the early New England migration into
Ohio; and some of their rural charm was carried, at
a later stage, into Wisconsin. In the group of villages that forms the Amana Colony in Iowa, the most
sturdy and economically successful of religious utopias
after those of the Shakers, the original terms of the
medieval village were handsomely carried forward into
the twentieth century. Some of their essential form
will underlie every sound modern plan for a life that
brings together rural and urban functions, not to say
felicities.

CHAPTER TWO

THE HERITAGE OF THE RENAISSANCE

THE forces that undermined the medieval civilization of Europe sapped the vitality from the little
centers it had deposited in America. What happened
in the course of three or four centuries in Europe
took scarcely a hundred years on this side of the
Atlantic.

Economically and culturally, the village community had been pretty well self-contained; it scraped
along on its immediate resources, and if it could not
purchase for itself the "best of everything" it at
least made the most of what it had. In every detail of house construction, from the setting of fireplaces to the slope of the roof, there were local peculiarities which distinguished not merely the Dutch
settlements from the English, but which even characterized several settlements in Rhode Island that were
scarcely a day's tramp apart. The limitation of
materials, and the carpenter's profound ignorance
of "style" made for freedom and diversity. It re-

mained for the eighteenth century to erect a single
canon of taste.

With the end of the seventeenth century the economic basis of provincial life shifted from the farm
to the sea. This change had the same effect upon
New England, where the village-community proper
alone had flourished, that fur-trading had had upon
New York: it broke up the internal unity of the
village by giving separate individuals the opportunity by what was literally a "lucky haul," to
achieve a position of financial superiority. Fisher-
men are the miners of the water. Instead of the
long, watchful care that the farmer must exercise
from planting time to harvest, fishing demands a
sharp eye and a quick, hard stroke of work; and
since what the Germans call *Sitzfleisch* is not one of
the primary qualities of a free lad, it is no wonder
that the sea weaned the young folks of New England away from the drudgeries of its boulder-strewn
farms. With fishing, trading, and building wooden
vessels for sale in foreign ports, riches poured into
maritime New England; and what followed scarcely
needs an explanation.

These villages ceased to be communities of farmers, working the land and standing squarely on their

own soil: they became commercial towns which, instead of trading for a living, simply lived for trade. With this change, castes arose; first, the division between the poor and the rich, and then between craftsmen and merchants, between the independent workers and the menials. The common concerns of all the townsfolk took second rank: the privileges of the great landlords and merchants warped the development of the community. Boston, by the middle of the eighteenth century, was rich in public buildings, including four schoolhouses, seventeen churches, a Town House, a Province House, and Faneuil Hall—a pretty large collection for a town whose twenty thousand inhabitants would scarcely fill a single block of tenements in the Bronx. But by this time a thousand inhabitants were set down as poor, and an almshouse and a workhouse had been provided for them.

With the rise of the merchant class, the industrial guild began to weaken, as it had weakened in Europe during the Renaissance. For about a hundred years the carpenter-builder continued to remain on the scene, and work in his forthright and painstaking and honest manner; but in the middle of the eighteenth century he was joined, for the

first time, by the professional architect, the first one
being probably Peter Harrison, who designed the
Redwood Library, which still stands in Newport.
Under competition with architects and amateurs of
taste, the carpenter-builder lost his position as an
independent craftsman, building intelligently for his
equals: he was forced to meet the swift, corrosive
influences brought in from foreign lands by men
who had visited the ports of the world; and he must
set his sails in order to catch the new winds of
fashion.

What were these winds, and what effect did they
have upon the architecture of the time?

Most of the influences that came by way of trade
affected only the accent of architecture; the language remained a homely vernacular. In the middle
of the eighteenth century China sent over wall-
paper; and in the Metropolitan Museum there is an
American lacquered cabinet dated as early as 1700,
decorated with obscure little Chinese figures in
gilded gesso. "China" itself came in to take the
place of pewter and earthenware in the finer
houses; while in the gardens of the great manors,
pavilions and pagodas, done more or less in the
Chinese manner, were fashionable. Even Thomas

Jefferson, with his impeccably classical taste, designed such a pavilion for Monticello before the Revolution.

This specific Chinese influence was part of that large, eclectic Oriental influence of the eighteenth century. The cultural spirit that produced Montesquieu's Lettres Persanes also led to the translation of the Chinese and Persian and Sanskrit classics, and by a more direct route brought home Turkish dressing-gowns, turbans, and slippers to Boston merchants. In Copley's painting of Nicholas Boylston, in 1767, these Turkish ornaments rise comically against the suggestion of a Corinthian pillar in the background; and this pillar recalls to us the principal influence of the time—that of classic civilization. This influence entered America first as a motif in decoration, and passed out only after it had become a dominating motive in life.

II

The Renaissance was an orientation of the European mind towards the forms of Roman and Greek civilization, and towards the meaning of classical culture. On the latter side its impulse was plainly a liberating one: it delivered the human soul from a cell of torments in which there were no modulating interests or activities between the base satisfactions of the temporal life and the beatitudes of heaven. With the Renaissance the god-beast became, once again, a man. Moreover, just when the Catholic culture of Christendom was breaking down under the influence of heresy and skepticism, the classics brought to the educated men of Europe a common theme which saved them from complete intellectual vagrancy. The effect of classical civilization, on the other hand, was not an unmixed good: for it served all too quickly to stereotype in old forms a spirit which had been freshly reborn, and it set up a servile principle in the arts which has in part been responsible for the wreck of both taste and craftsmanship.

The first builders of the Renaissance, in Italy, were not primarily architects; they were rather supreme artists in the minor crafts; and their chief failing was, perhaps, that they wished to stamp with their personal imprint all the thousand details of sculpture, painting, and carving which had hitherto been left to the humble craftsman. Presently, the technical knowledge of the outward treatment of a building became a touchstone to success; and a literal understanding of the products of antiquity took the place in lesser men of personal inspiration. The result was that architecture became more and more a thing of paper designs and exact archæological measurements; the workman was condemned to carry out in a faithful, slavish way the details which the architect himself had acquired in similar fashion. So the architect ceased to be a master-builder working among comrades of wide experience and travel: he became a Renaissance gentleman who merely gave orders to his servants.

Victor Hugo said in Notre Dame that the printing-press destroyed architecture, which had hitherto been the stone record of mankind. The real misdemeanor of the printing-press, however, was not that it took literary values away from architecture, but that it caused architecture to derive its value from literature. With the Renaissance the great modern distinction between the literate and the illiterate extends even to building; the master mason who knew his stone and his workmen and his tools and the tradition of his art gave way to the architect who knew his Palladio and his Vignola and his Vitruvius. Architecture, instead of striving to

leave the imprint of a happy spirit on the super-
ficies of a building, became a mere matter of grammatical accuracy and pronunciation; and the seventeenth-century architects who revolted from this
regime and created the baroque were at home only
in the pleasure gardens and theaters of princes. For
the common run of architects, particularly in the
northern countries, the Five Orders became as un-
challengeable as the eighty-one rules of Latin syn-
tax. To build with a pointed arch was barbarous,
to build with disregard for formal symmetry was
barbarous, to permit the common workman to carry
out his individual taste in carving was to risk vul-
garity and pander to an obsolete sense of democracy.
The classics had, it is true, united Europe anew in
a catholic culture; but alas! it was only the leisured
upper classes who could fully take possession of the
new kingdom of the mind. The Five Orders remained firmly entrenched on one side, the "lower
orders" on the other.

Hereafter, architecture lives by the book. First
it is Palladio and Vignola; then it is Burlington and
Chambers; then, after the middle of the eighteenth
century, the brothers Adam and Stuart's Antiquities of Athens. Simpler works with detailed pre-

scriptions for building in the fashionable mode made
their way in the late seventeenth century among the
smaller fry of carpenters and builders; and they
were widely used in America, as a guide to taste and
technique, right down to the middle of the nineteenth
century. It was by means of the book that the
architecture of the eighteenth century from St.
Petersburg to Philadelphia seemed cast by a single
mind. We call the mode Georgian because vast
quantities of such building was done in England,
as a result of the general commercial prosperity of
that country; but it was common wherever European
civilization had any fresh architectural effort to
make, and if we call this style "colonial" in America
it is not to mark any particular lapse or lack of
distinction.

The Renaissance in architecture had reached
England at about the time of the Great Fire (1666),
fully two generations after the Italian influence had
made its way into English literature; and it came
to America, as one might guess, about a generation
later. It was left for Alexander Pope, who himself
was a dutiful Augustan, to sum up the situation
with classic precision to Lord Burlington, who had
published Palladio's Antiquities of Rome:

"You show us Rome was glorious, not profuse,
And pompous buildings once were things of use.
Yet shall, my lord, your just and noble rules
Fill half the land with imitation fools;
Who random drawings from your sheets shall take
And of one beauty many blunders make."

These lines were a warning and a prophecy. The warning was timely; and the prophecy came true, except in those districts in which the carpenter continued to ply his craft without the overlordship of the architect.

III

The first effect of the Renaissance forms in America was not to destroy the vernacular but to perfect it; for it provided the carpenter-builder, whose distance from Europe kept him from profiting by the spirited work of his forbears, with a series of ornamental motifs. New England, under the influence of an idol-breaking Puritanism, had been singularly poor in decoration, as I have already observed: its modest architectural effects relied solely on mass, color, and a nice disposition of parts. In its decorative aspects medievalism had left but a trace in

America: the carved grotesque heads on the face of the Van Cortlandt Mansion in New York, and the painted decorations in some of the older houses and barns among the Pennsylvania Dutch pretty well complete the tally.

Classical motifs served to fill the blank in provincial architecture. As long as the carpenter worked by himself, the classic influence was confined to little details like the fanlights, the moldings, the pillars of the portico, and so on. In the rural districts of New England, from Maine to Connecticut, and in certain parts of New York and New Jersey and Pennsylvania, the carpenter keeps on building in his solid, traditional manner down to the time that the jig-saw overwhelms a mechanically hypnotized age; and even through the jig-saw period in the older regions, the proportions and the plan remained close to tradition. The classical did not in fact supplant the vernacular until the last vestiges of the guild and the village-community had passed away, and the economic conditions appropriate to the Renaissance culture had made their appearance.

The dwelling house slowly became more habitable during this period: the skill in shipbuilding which every sheltered inlet gave evidence of was carried back into the home, and in the paneling of the walls and the general tidiness and compactness of the apartments, a shipshape order comes more and more to prevail. The plastered ceiling makes its appearance, and the papered wall; above all, white paint is introduced on the inside and outside of the house.

Besides giving more light, this innovation surely indicates that chimney flues had become more satisfactory. Paint was no doubt introduced to keep the torrid summer sun from charring the exposed clapboards; and white paint was used, despite the expense of white lead, for the reason that it accorded with the chaste effect which was inseparable in the eighteenth-century mind from classic precedent.

Indeed, the whiteness of our colonial architecture is an essential characteristic; it dazzled Dickens on his first visit to America, and made him think that all the houses had been built only yesterday. The esthetic reason for delighting in these white colonial farmhouses is simple: white and white alone fully reflects the surrounding lights; white and white alone gives a pure blue or lavender shadow against the sunlight. At dawn, a white house is pale pink and turquoise; at high noon it is clear yellow and lavender-blue; in a ripe sunset it is orange and purple; in short, except on a gray day it is anything but white. These old white houses, if they seem a little sudden and sharp in the landscape, are at least part of the sky: one finds them stretched on a slight rise above the highroad like a seagull with poised wings, or a cloud above the treetops. Were anything needed to make visible the deterioration of American life which the nineteenth century brought with it, the habit of painting both wood and brick gray should perhaps be sufficient.

III

If the architecture of the early eighteenth century in America is a little prim and angular, if it never rises far above a sturdy provincialism, it is not without its own kind of interest; and Faneuil Hall, for example, is not the worst of Boston's buildings, though it is overshadowed by the great utilitarian hulks that line the streets about it. By studying the classical forms at one remove, the builders of the eighteenth century in America had the same kind of advantage that Wren had in England. Wren's "Renaissance" churches, with their box-like naves and their series of superimposed orders for

steeples, of course, had many parallels in Italy
— but they certainly had no likeness to anything
that had been built in classic times: they were the
products of a playful and original fancy, like the
mermaid. Mere knowledge, mere imitation, would
never have achieved Renaissance architecture; it was
the very imperfection of the knowledge and dis-
cipleship that made it the appropriate shell of its
age. Coming to America in handbooks and prints,
chastely rendered, the models of antiquity were,
down to the Revolution, followed just so far as they
conveniently served. Instead of curbing invention,
they gave it a more definite problem to work upon.

It was a happy accident that made the carpenter-
builders and cabinet makers of America see their
China, their Paris, their Rome through a distance,
dimly. What those who admire the eighteenth century style do not, perhaps, see is that an accident
cannot be recovered. However painstakingly we
may cut the waistcoat, the stock, the knee-breeches
of an eighteenth-century costume, it is now only a
fancy dress: its "moment" in history is over. The
same principle holds true for Georgian or colonial
architecture, even more than it does for that of the
seventeenth century; for one might, indeed, con-

ceive of a breakdown in the transportation system or the credit system which would force a builder to rely for a while upon the products of his own region; whereas, while our civilization remains intact there are a hundred handbooks, measured drawings, and photographs which make a naïve recovery of antiquity impossible.

Once we have genuinely appreciated the influence that created early colonial architecture, we see that it is irrecoverable: what we call a revival is really a second burial. All the king's horses and all the king's men have been hauling and tugging vigorously during the last fifty years to bring back the simple beauties and graces of the colonial dwelling, and the collectors' hunt for the products of the Salem, Newburyport and Philadelphia cabinetmakers is a long and merry one; but the only beneficent effect of this movement has been the preservation of a handful of antiquities, which would otherwise have been impiously torn down. What we have built in the colonial mode is all very well in its way: unfortunately, it bears the same relation to the work of the late seventeenth and early eighteenth centuries that the Woolworth Building bears to the cathedrals of the Middle Age, or the patriotism of the National

Security League to the principles of Franklin and Jefferson. Photographic accuracy, neatly touched up—this is its capital virtue, and plainly, it has precious little to do with a living architecture. Like the ruined chapel in The Pirates of Penzance, our modern colonial houses are often attached to ancestral estates that were established—a year ago; and if their occupants are "descendants by purchase," what shall we say of their architects?

If any further proof of this were needed, the recent restoration of Williamsburg, Virginia, would be sufficient. This painstaking work of reconstruction, which has not merely re-created the old buildings but also put them under the custodianship of people dressed in the costume of the period, has all the merits of a great open air museum, except one: it leaves nothing to the imagination. As an educational instrument, it has many invaluable features; but perhaps its greatest lesson is finally this—the past cannot be re-presented in space because one element is missing, time, which brings changes and transformations. If even a museum laboriously counterfeiting the past has this quaintly unauthentic look, accentuated by the colonial A & P store just around the corner, how could one hope for anything closer to reality in a living community?

CHAPTER THREE

THE CLASSICAL MYTH

THE transformation of European society and its
material shell that took place during the period we
call the Renaissance is associated with the break-up
of the town economy and its replacement by a mer-
cantile economy devoted to the advantage of the
State. Along with this goes the destruction of the
village community, and the predominance in social
affairs of a landholding oligarchy who have thrown
off feudal responsibilities while they have retained
most of the feudal privileges, and a merchant class,
buttressed by riches derived from war, piracy, and
sharp trade.

America reproduced in miniature the changes that
were taking place in Europe. Because of its isola-
tion and the absence of an established social order,
it showed these changes without the blur and con-
fusion that attended them abroad.

It is sometimes a little difficult to tell whether
the classical modes of building were a result of
these changes in society or, among other things, an

incentive to them; whether the classical frame fitted the needs of the time, or whether men's activities expanded to occupy the idolum that had seized their imagination. At any rate, the notion that the classical taste in architecture developed mainly through technical interests in design will not hold; for the severely classical shell arose only in regions where the social conditions had laid a foundation for the classical myth.

The first development of the grand style in the American renaissance was in the manors of Virginia and Maryland. It came originally through an imitation of the country houses of England, and then, after the Revolutionary War, it led to a direct adaptation of the Roman villa and the Greek temple. One does not have to go very deep to fetch up the obvious parallel between the land-monopoly and slavery that prevailed in the American manors and the conditions that permitted the Roman villa itself to assume its stately proportions; nor need one dwell too long upon the natural subordination, in this regime, of the carpenter-builder to the gentleman-architect. "In the town palaces and churches," as Mr. Fiske Kimball justly says, "there was a strong contradiction between modern conditions and ancient forms, so that it was only in the country that Palladio's ideas of domestic architecture could come to a clear and successful expression. These monuments, since so much neglected, served in Palladio's book expressly to represent the 'Antients' designs of country-houses. . . .' "

At his death, Robert Carter, who had been Rector of the College, Speaker of the Burgesses, President of the Council, Acting Governor of Virginia, and Proprietor of the Northern Neck, was described in the Gentleman's Magazine of 1732 as the possessor of an estate of 300,000 acres of land, about 1,000 slaves, and ten thousand pounds. Pliny the Younger might well have been proud of such an estate. On a substantial basis like this, a Palladian mansion was possible; and up and down the land, wherever the means justified the end, Palladian mansions were built.

The really striking thing about the architecture of Manorial America with its great dignity and its sometimes striking beauty of detail or originality of design—as in the staircase at Berry Hill which creates a flaring pattern like butterfly's wings—the striking thing is the fact that the work is not the product of a specialized education; it is rather the outcome of a warm, loving, and above all intelligent commerce with the past, in the days before Horseback Hall had become as aimless and empty as Heartbreak House. Mr. Arthur T. Bolton, the biographer of the brothers Adam, has exhibited letters from Robert Adam's patrons in England which mark their avid and precise interest in classical forms; and without doubt a little digging would uncover similar examples in America.

These educated eighteenth-century gentlemen, these contemporaries of "Junius" and Gibbon, who had read Horace and Livy and Plutarch, had one foot in their own age, and the other in the grave of Rome. In America, Thomas Jefferson exemplified this whole culture at its best and gave it a definite stamp: he combined in almost equal degrees the statesman, the student, and the artist. Not merely did Jefferson design his own Monticello; he executed a number of other houses for the surrounding gentry —Shadwell, Edgehill, Farrington—to say nothing of the Virginia State Capitol and the church and university at Charlottesville. It was Jefferson who in America first gave a strict interpretation to classicism; for he had nothing but contempt for the free, Georgian vernacular which was making its

PLATE THREE   Monticello, Virginia. Thomas Jefferson, architect. (1796-1805)

way among those who regarded the classical past as little more than a useful embellishment.

The contrast between the classical and the vernacular, between the architecture of the plantation and the architecture of the village, between the work of the craftsman, and the work of the gentleman and the professional architect, became even more marked after the Revolutionary War. As a result of that re-crystallization of American society, the conditions of classical culture and classical civilization were for a short time fused in the activities of the community, even in the town. One may express the transformation in a crude way by saying that the carpenter-builder had been content with a classical finish; the architects of the early republic worked upon a classical foundation. It was the Revolution itself, I believe, that turned the classical taste into a myth which had the power to move men and mold their actions.

The merchant who has spent his hours in the counting house and on the quay cannot with the most lofty effort convert himself into a classical hero. It is different with men who have spent long nights and days wrangling in the State House, men who have ridden on horseback through a campaign, men

who have plotted like Catiline and denounced like
Cicero, men whose daily actions are governed with
the fine resolution of a Roman general or dictator.
Unconsciously, such men want a stage to set off
and magnify their actions. King Alfred can perhaps remain a king, though he stays in a cottage
and minds the cakes on the griddle; but most of us
need a little scenery and ritual to confirm these high
convictions. If the tailors had not produced the
frock-coat, Daniel Webster would have had to invent
one. The merchant wants his little comforts and
conveniences; at most, he desires the architect to
make his gains conspicuous; but the hero who has
drawn his sword or addressed an assembly wants
elbow room for gestures. His parlor must be big
enough for a public meeting, his dining room for a
banquet. So it follows that whereas under pre-
Revolutionary conventions even civic buildings like
Independence Hall in Philadelphia are built on a
domestic scale, the early republican architecture is
marked by the practice of building its domestic
dwellings on a public scale. The fine houses of the
early republic all have an official appearance; almost
any house might be the White House.

Even when Dickens made his first visit to America,

the classical myth and the classical hero had not
altogether disappeared: one has a painful memory
of the "mother of the modern Gracchi," and one
sees how the republican hero had been vulgarized
into a Jacksonian caricature like General Cyrus
Choke. For a whole generation the classical myth
held men in its thrall; the notion of returning to a
pagan polity, quaintly modified by deism, was a
weapon of the radical forces in both America and
France. Jean Jacques himself preached the virtues
of Sparta and Rome in Le Contrat Social, as well
as the state of nature which he praised in Emile;
and, in general, "radicalism" associated itself with
the worship of rule and reason, as opposed to the
caprice, the irrationality, the brute traditionalism
of what the children of that age then characterized
as "Gothic superstition." Almost within his lifetime Washington became Divus Cæsar, and if a monument was not built to him immediately, a city was
named after him, as Alexandria had been named
after Alexander. Did not the very war-veterans become the Society of the Cincinnati; did not the first
pioneers on the westward march sprinkle names like
Utica and Ithaca and Syracuse over the Mohawk
trail; and did not a few ex-soldiers go back to their

Tory neighbor's plow? As Rome and Greece embodied the political interests of the age, so did classical architecture provide the appropriate shell. Even those who were not vitally touched by the dominant interests of the period were not immune to the fashion, once it had been set.

II

In New England, not unnaturally, the influence of the merchant prevailed in architecture for a longer time, perhaps, than it did elsewhere. Samuel McIntire, a carver of figureheads for ships and moldings for cabins, provided an interior setting in the fashion of Robert Adam, which enabled the merchant of Salem to live like a lord in Berkeley Square; and Bulfinch, a merchant's son, began by repairing his father's house, went on a grand tour of Europe, and returned to a lucrative practice which included the first monument on Bunker Hill, and the first theater opened in Boston. Under McIntire's assiduous and scholarly hands, the low-lying traditional farmhouse was converted into the bulky square house with its hipped roof, its classical pilasters, its frequently ill-proportioned cupola, its "captain's walk," or "widow's walk." The merchant with his eye for magnitude lords it over the farmer with his homely interest in the wind and the weather; and so McIntire, the last great figure in a dying line of craftsmen-artists, is compelled to make up by wealth of ornament a beauty which the earlier provincial houses had achieved by adaptation to the site without, and to subtlety of proportion within. The standard of conspicuous waste, as Mr. Thorstein Veblen would call it, spread from the manor to the city mansion.

Throughout the rest of the country, the pure classical myth created the mold of American architecture, and buildings that were not informed by this myth attempted some sort of mimicry, like the mansion Squire Jones built for Marmaduke Temple in Cooper's The Pioneers. There are churches standing in New Jersey and New York, for example, built as late as 1850, which at a distance have the outlines and proportions of classic buildings, either in the earlier style of Wren, or in the more severe and stilted Greek manner favored by a later generation. It is only on closer inspection that one discovers that the ornament has become an illiterate reminiscence; that the windows are bare openings; that the orders have lost their proportions, and that, unlike the wandering mechanic, who "with a few soiled plates of English architecture" helped Squire Jones, the builder could no longer pretend to talk learnedly "of friezes, entablatures, and particularly of the composite order." Alas for a bookish architecture when the taste for reading disappears!

III

The dominant designs of the early republican period proceeded directly or indirectly from such books as Stuart's Antiquities of Athens, and from such well-known examples of temple architecture in southern Europe as the Maison Carrée at Nîmes. In one sense, there was a certain fitness in adapting the Greek methods of building to America. Originally, the Greek temple had probably been a wooden building. Its columns were trees, its cornices exposed beams; and the fact that in America one could again build mightily in wood may have furnished an extra incentive to the erection of these colossal buildings. The fact that the Greek mode in America was well under way before the first example of it had appeared in Edinburgh, London, or Paris, shows perhaps that time and place both favored its introduction on this side of the Atlantic: for the availability of certain materials often, no doubt, directs the imagination to certain forms.

On the whole, however, the Greek temple precedent was a bad one. For one thing, since the Greek *cella* had no source of light except the doorway, it was necessary to introduce modifications in the elevation, and to break up the interior; and it was only in the South that the vast shadowed retreats formed by porches and second-story balconies proved a happy adaptation to the climate. Again: Greek architecture was an architecture of exteriors, designed for people who spent the greater part of the year out of doors. With no temple ritual comparable to the services of the church or cathedral, the Greeks lavished their attention upon externals, and as a great admirer of the Greeks, Sir Reginald Blomfield well says, "may have been more successful with the outside of their buildings than with the inside." To fail with the interior in a northern climate is to fail with the essentials of a habitation; and these vast rooms, for all their ornament, too often remained bleak.

Even on the esthetic side, the Greek style of building was not a full-blown success. With all their
strict arrangement of the classic orders, with all
their nice proportions, the muted white exteriors
resembled a genuine Greek temple in the way that a
sepia photograph would represent a sunrise—the
warm tones, the colors, the dancing procession of
sculptures were absent; it was a thinned and watered
Greece that they called to mind. Indeed, the disciples of the Age of Reason and white perukes would
have been horrified, I have no doubt, at the "barbarism" of the original Greek temples, as they would
doubtless also have been at the meanness of the
dwellings in which Pericles or Thucydides must have
lived. Once the temple-house ceased to be a stage
upon which the myth of classicism could be enacted,
it ceased also to be a home. For who wishes to
live in a temple? That is a spiritual exercise we
do not demand even of a priest. Small wonder that
the temple lingered longest in the South, where,
down to the Civil War, gangs of slaves supported the
dignity of the masters and a large household dimin-
ished the chilly sense of solitude.

It was in public architecture that the early
republic succceded best, and it was here that its

influence lingered longest, for down to 1840 well-designed buildings in the classic mode, like the Sub-Treasury building in New York, were still put up. The work of McComb in New York, Hoadley in Connecticut, Latrobe in Pennsylvania and Maryland, to mention only a few of the leading architects, represents the high-water mark of professional design in America; and the fact that in spite of the many hands that worked upon it the Capitol at Washington is still a fairly coherent structure is a witness to the strength of their tradition. For all its minor felicities, however, we must not make the mistake of the modern revivalists, like Mr. Fiske Kimball, who urge the acceptance of the classic tradition in America as a foundation for a general modern style. Form and function are too far divorced in the classic mode to permit the growth of an architecture which will proceed on all fours in houses and public buildings, and factories and barns; moreover, there are too many new structures in the modern world which the builders of Rome or the Renaissance have not even dimly anticipated. In medieval building the town hall is a different sort of building from the cathedral: using the same elements, perhaps, it nevertheless contrives an altogether different effect. In the architecture of the early republic, on the other hand, the treasury building might be a church, and the church might be a mansion, for any external differentiation one can observe—in fact, the only ecclesiastical feeling that goes with the churches of the time is a cold deism, or an equally cold Protestant faith which has lost entirely the memories and associations of the intervening centuries. This sort of architecture achieves order and dignity, not by composing differences, but by canceling them. Its standards do not inhere in the building, but are laid on outside of it. When the purpose of the structure happens to conform to the style, the result may be admirable in every way. When it does not happen to conform the result is tedious and banal; and, to tell the truth, a great deal of the architecture of the early republic is tedious and banal.

IV

One further effect of the classic mode has still to be noted: the introduction of formal city design, by the French engineer, Major L'Enfant, in the laying out of Washington. Stirred by the memory of

PLATE FOUR   *The L'Enfant plan for Washington,
D. C. (1791)*

the grand design of Paris under Louis XIV, with its radiating avenues that cut through the city in the way that riding lanes cut through the hunting forest, L'Enfant sought to superimpose a dignified pattern upon the rectangular plan provided by the commissioners of Washington. By putting the major public buildings in key positions, by providing for a proper physical relation between the various departments of the government, by planning spacious avenues of approach, culminating in squares, triangles, and round-points, Major L'Enfant gave great dignity to the new capital city, and even though in the years that followed his plan was often ignored and overridden, it still maintained a monumental framework for the administrative buildings of the American State.

Unfortunately, if Washington has the coherence of a formal plan, it also has its abstractness: contrived to set off and serve the buildings of the government, it exercised no control over domestic building, over business, over the manifold economic functions of the developing city. The framework was excellent, if cities could live by government alone. By laying too much stress on formal order, the exponents of classic taste paved the way for the all too formal order of the gridiron plan, and since the gridiron development was suited to hasty commercial exploitation, while the mode of Washington was not, it was in this mold that the architecture of the nineteenth century was cast.

Within a short while after its introduction in New York in 1811 the effects of the rectangular streets and rectangular lots became evident; whereas the prints of New York before 1825 show a constant variety in the elevation and layout of houses, those after this date resemble more and more standardized boxes. Long monotonous streets that terminated nowhere, filled by rows of monotonous houses—this was the net contribution of the formal plan. Classical taste was not responsible for these enormities—but on the whole it did nothing to check them, and since the thrifty merchants of New York could not understand L'Enfant's plan for Washington, they seized upon that part of it which was intelligible: its regularity, its appearance of order.

With the new forces that were at work on the American scene, with the disintegration of classical culture under the combined influence of pioneer enterprise, mechanical invention, overseas commerce, and the almost religious cult of utilitarianism, all this was indeed inevitable. What happened to the proud, Roman-patterned republic of 1789 is a matter of common knowledge. Benjamin Latrobe, the British architect who contributed so much to the Capitol at Washington—including a new order of corn stalks and tobacco leaves—was a witness to the disintegration of the age and the dissolution of its world of ideas; and there is a familiar ring to his commentary upon it:

"I remember [he says in his autobiography] the time when I was over head and ears in love with Man in a State of Nature. . . . Social Compacts were my hobbies; the American Revolution—I ask its pardon, for it deserves better company—was a sort of dream of the Golden Age; and the French Revolution was the Golden Age itself. I should be ashamed to confess all this if I had not a thousand companions in my kaleidoscopic amusement, and those generally men of ardent, benevolent, and well-informed minds and excellent hearts. Alas! experience has destroyed the illusion, the kaleidoscope is broken, and all the tinsel of scenery that glittered so delightfully is translated and turned to raggedness. A dozen years' residence at the Republican court of

Washington had affected wonderfully the advance of riper years."

Major L'Enfant's plan for Washington was the last gasp, it seems to me, of the classical order; Jefferson's University of Virginia was perhaps its most perfect consummation, for Jefferson had planned for the life of the institution as well as for the shell which was to contain it. Before the nineteenth century was long under way men's minds ceased to move freely within the classical idolum; and by 1860 the mood was obliterated and a large part of the work had been submerged or destroyed. The final ironic commentary upon the dignity and austerity of the earlier temples is illustrated in a house in Kennebunkport, Maine; for there the serene, pillared façade is broken up in the rear by a later, and alas! a necessary addition: a two-story bow-window projected far enough beyond the eaves to give a little light to the occupants of the rooms!

In sum, there was a pathetic incompatibility in this architecture between need and achievement, between pretensions and matter-of-fact—a rigid opposition to common sense that a vernacular, however playful, would never countenance. These temples

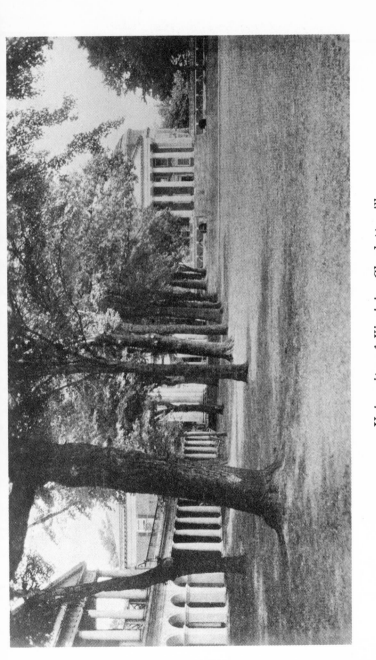

PLATE FIVE *University of Virginia. Charlottesville, Va. Thomas Jefferson, architect.*

were built with the marmoreal gesture of eternity; they satisfied the desire and fashion of the moment; and today their ghosts parade before us, brave but incredible.

Strangely enough, the one group of buildings that had universal elements that transcended its would-be classicism, the University of Virginia, remained unimitated, indeed almost unperceived, during the next century. Jefferson's bold precedents, both as an organizer of a living university and as the creative designer of fresh spatial compositions, which owed nothing to medieval quadrangles and little to baroque palace design, were completely ignored in the layouts of new colleges and universities. Even in the later university buildings at Charlottesville, Jefferson's masterly precedents were as wantonly flouted as Frederick Law Olmsted's superb master-plan was ignored, after the original spate of building, at Stanford. Had Jefferson's masterpiece been understood, had its innovations in row-planning, which went beyond the best work of the Nash's in Bath, been assimilated, the history of urban design in America would have been radically different—and better.

CHAPTER FOUR

THE DIASPORA OF THE PIONEER

FROM the standpoint of architecture, the early part of the nineteenth century was a period of disintegration. The gap between sheer utility and art, which the Renaissance had emphasized, was widened with the coming of machinery. That part of architecture which was touched by industrialism became crude beyond belief: the new mills and factories were usually packing boxes, lacking in light and ventilation, and the homes of the factory workers, when they were not the emptied houses of merchants and tradesmen, made to serve a dozen families instead of the original one, were little more than covered pens, as crowded as a cattle market. At the same time that the old forms were undermined by the new methods of mechanical production, a sentimental longing to retain those forms, just because they were old, seized men's minds; and so industrialism and romanticism divided the field of architecture between them.

It was no accident that caused romanticism and industrialism to appear at the same time. They were rather the two faces of the new civilization, one looking towards the past, and the other towards the future; one glorifying the new, the other clinging to the old; industrialism intent on increasing the physical means of subsistence, romanticism living in a sickly fashion on the hollow glamour of the past. The age not merely presented these two aspects; it sought to enjoy each of them. Where industrialism took root, the traditions of architecture were disregarded; where romanticism flourished, on the other hand, in the mansions, public buildings, and churches, architecture became capricious and absurd, and it returned to a past that had never existed. Against the gross callousness which a Bounderby exhibited toward beauty and amenity, there was only the bland piety of a Pecksniff.

The dream that is dying and the dream that is coming to birth do not stand in sequence, but mingle as do the images in a dissolving view; and during the very years that the architecture of the Renaissance, both in Europe and America, achieved new heights of formal design, the first factories were being planted in Staffordshire and Yorkshire, the Duke of Bridgewater built his famous canal, and Horace Walpole designed his "Gothic" mansion on Straw-

berry Hill. The coincidence of industrialism and
romanticism is just as emphatic in America as in
England; and it is not without historic justice that
the architect who in 1807 designed the chapel of St.
Mary's Seminary in Baltimore, after the Gothic
fashion, successfully introduced a steam pumping
system in Philadelphia's waterworks. While the
industrial buildings of the period represented nothing but a lapse from the current vernacular, due to
haste and insufficient resources, romantic architecture was a positive influence; and it will perhaps best
serve our purpose to examine the romantic heritage
in its pristine form, rather than in the work of disciples like Latrobe, whose American practice is dated
about two generations later.

The author of The Castle of Otranto had a per-
verse and wayward interest in the past; and the
spirit he exhibited in both his novel and his country
home was typical of the romantic attitude everywhere. What attracted Walpole to the Gothic style
was little more than the phosphorescence of decay:
he summoned up the ghosts of the Middle Ages but
not the guilds; and instead of admiring the sound-
ness of medieval masonry, those who followed directly
in his path were affected rather by the spectacle of

its dilapidation, so that the production of authentic ruins became one of the chief efforts of the eighteenth-century landscape gardener.

It is not a great step from building a ruin to building a mansion that is little better than a ruin. While Walpole defended Strawberry Hill by saying he did not aim to make his house so Gothic as to exclude convenience, it happened again and again that the picturesque was the enemy of simple honesty and necessity; and just as Walpole himself in his refectory used wall paper that imitated stucco, so did other owners and builders use plaster and hangings and wall paper and carpet to cover up defects of construction. Towers that no one ever climbed, turrets that no one could enter, and battlements that no one rose to defend, took the place of the classic orders. The drawbridge-and-moat that embellished Mr. Wemmick's villa in Great Expectations was not a wild conceit of Dickens but a relic of Walpole and his successors.

As a disguise for mean or thoughtless workmanship, the application of antique "style" was the romantic contribution to architecture; and it served very handily during the period of speculative building and selling that accompanied the growth of the new industrial towns. Even where style did not conceal commercial disingenuousness, it covered up a poverty of imagination in handling the elements of a building. Gothic touches about doors and the exterior of windows, and a heap of bric-a-brac and curios on the inside, softened the gauntness and bareness of this architecture, or rather, distracted attention from them. Curiosity was the dominant mood of the time, acquisitiveness its principal impulse, and comfort its end. Many good things doubtless came out of this situation; but architecture was not one of them.

II

Modern industrialism began to take root in America after the War of Independence, and its effect was twofold: it started up new villages which centered about the waterfall or the iron mine and had scarcely any other concern than industry; at the same time, by cutting canals which tapped the interior, it drew life away from the smaller provincial ports and concentrated commerce and population in great towns like Boston, Philadelphia, and New York. In New England, as in the English

Cotswolds from Witney to Chalford, the mechanical regime was humanized by the presence of an
older civilization, and the first generation of factory
hands were farmers' lads and lasses who neither lost
nor endangered their independence; but where the
factory depended upon paupers or immigrants, as
it did in the big towns and in some of the unsettled
parts of the country, the community relapsed into
a barbarism which affected the masters as well as
the hands. There was more than a difference in
literary taste between the Corinths and Bethels named
by an earlier generation and the Mechanicsvilles that
followed them.

The chief watchwords of the time were progress
and expansion. The first belonged to the pioneer
in industry who opened up new areas for mechanical
invention and applied science; the second, to the land
pioneer; and between these two resourceful types
the old ways, were they good or bad, were scrapped,
and the new ways, were they good or bad, were
adopted. Both land pioneering and industrial
pioneering were essentially subdivisions of one occu-
pation, mining; and, following the clue opened by
Messrs. Geddes and Branford, one may say with
Professor Adshead that the nineteenth century

witnessed "the great attack of the miner on the peasant."

Mechanical industry owes its great development and progress to the work of the woodman and the miner: the first type of worker takes the bent sapling and develops the lathe or "bodger" which is still to be found in the remote parts of the Chiltern Hills in England, while from the mine itself not merely comes the steam engine, first used for pumping out water, but likewise the railway. The perpetual débris amid which the miner lives forms a capital contrast with the ordered culture, the careful weeding and cutting, of field and orchard: almost any sort of habitation is an advance upon the squalor of the pithead; and it is not a mere chance that the era devoted to mining and all its accessory manufactures was throughout the western world the dingiest and dirtiest that has yet befouled the earth. Choked by his own débris, or stirred by the exhaustion of minerals, the miner's community runs down—and he departs.

The name pioneer has a romantic color; but in America the land pioneer mined the forests and the soil, and the industry pioneer almost as ruthlessly mined the human resources, and when the pay-dirt got sallow and thin, they both moved on. Long-fellow's allusion to the "bivouac of life" unconsciously points to the prevailing temper; for even those who remained in the older American centers were affected by the pioneer's malaise and unsettlement; and they behaved as if at any moment they might be called to the colors and sent westward.

Beside the vivid promises of Mechanical Progress and Manifest Destiny the realities of an ordered society thinned into a pale vapor. In many little communities Mechanical Societies were formed for the propagation of the utilitarian faith: industrialism with its ascetic ritual of unsparing work, its practice of thrift, its renunciation of the arts, gathered to itself the religious zeal of Protestantism. The erection of factories, the digging of canals, the location of furnaces, the building of roads, the devising of inventions, not merely exhausted a great part of the available capital; even more, it occupied the energy and imagination of the more vigorous spirits. Two generations before, Thomas Jefferson could lay out and develop the estate of Monticello; now, with many of Jefferson's capacities, Poe could only dream about the fantastic Domain of Arnheim. The society around Poe had no more use for an architectural imagination than the Puritans had for decorative images; the smoke of the factory-chimney was incense, the scars on the landscape were as the lacerations of a saint, and the mere multiplication of gaunt sheds and barracks was a sign of progress, and therefore an earnest of perfection.

Did ever so many elements of disintegration come together at one time and place before? The absence of tradition and example raised enough difficulties in Birmingham and Manchester and Lyons and Essen; but in America it was accentuated by the restless march of those pioneers who, in the words of a contemporary economist, "leave laws, education and the arts, all the essential elements of civilization, behind them." What place could architecture fill in these squatter communities? It could diminish the hardships of living; it could grease the channels of gain; and it could demolish or "improve" so much of the old as it could not understand, as Bulfinch's Court House in Newburyport was improved, and as many a fine city residence was swept away under the tide of traffic.

These were the days when the log cabin flourished; but it did not remain long enough in place to become the well-wrought and decorative piece of rustic architecture that the better sort of peasant hut, done with the same materials, became in Russia. A genuine architectural development might have led from a crude log cabin to a finished one, from a bare cabin to an enriched and garnished one, and so, perhaps, in the course of a century or so, to a fine country architecture and a great native art of wood carving comparable to that of the Russian sculptors today. In America, however, the pioneer jumped baldly from log cabin to White House, or its genteel and scroll-sawed equivalent; and the arts inherent in good building never had a chance to develop. With the animus of the miner in back of everything the pioneer attempted, the pioneer's architecture was all false-work and scantling.

III

The first contribution to the pioneer's comfort was Franklin's ingenious stove (1745). After that came a number of material appliances. Central heating gave the American house a Roman standard of comfort, the astral-oil lamp captivated Edgar Poe; and cooking stoves, gas-lighting, permanent bathtubs, and water-closets made their way into the better sort of house in the Eastern cities before the middle of the nineteenth century. In the development of the city itself, the gridiron plan was added to the list of labor-saving devices. Although the gridiron plan had the same relation to natural conditions and fundamental social needs as a paper constitution has to the living customs of a people, the simplicity of the gridiron plan won the heart of the pioneer. Its rectangular blocks formed parcels of land which he could sell by the front foot and gamble with as easily as if he were playing cards, and deeds of transfer could be drawn up hastily with the same formula for each plot; moreover, the least competent surveyor, without thought or knowledge, could project the growth of New Eden's streets and avenues into an interminable future. In nineteenth-century city planning the engineer was the willing servant of the land monopolist; and he provided a frame for the architect—a frame in which we still struggle today—where site-value counted for everything, and sight-value was not even an afterthought.

In street layout and land subdivision no attention was paid to the final use to which the land would be put; but the most meticulous efforts were made to

safeguard its immediate use, namely, land-specula-
tion. In order to further this use hills were graded,
swamps and ponds filled, and streets laid out before
these expenditures could be borne by the people
who, in the end, were to profit by or suffer from
them. It was no wonder that the newer towns like
Cincinnati, St. Louis, and Chicago by the middle
of the century had forfeited to the gambler in real
estate, to pay the cost of street improvements, generous tracts of land which the original planners had
set aside as civic centers. Planned by men who still
retained some of the civic vision of the early republic, the commercial city speedily drifted into the
hands of people who had no more civic scruples than
the keeper of a lottery.

The gridiron plan had one other defect which
was accounted a virtue by the pioneer, and still is
shared by those who have not profited by the intervening century's experience. With its avenues that
encompassed swamps and wildernesses, with its
future growth forecast for at least a hundred years,
the complete city plan captivated the imagination.
Scarcely any American town was so mean that it
did not attempt to grow faster than its neighbor,
faster perhaps than New York. Only by the accu-

mulation of more and more people could its colossal city plan and its inflated land values be realized. If the older cities of the seaboard were limited in their attempts to become metropolises by the fact that their downtown sections were originally laid out for villages, the villages of the middle west labored under just the opposite handicap; they had frequently acquired the framework of a metropolis before they had passed out of the physical state of a village. The gridiron plan was a sort of hand-me-down which the juvenile city was supposed to grow into and fill. That a city had any other purpose than to attract trade, to increase land values, and to grow is something that, if it uneasily entered the mind of an occasional Whitman, never exercised any hold upon the minds of the majority of our countrymen. For them, the place where the great city stands *is* the place of stretched wharves, and markets, and ships bringing goods from the ends of the earth; that, and nothing else.

IV

With business booming and vanishing, with people coming and going, with land continually changing hands, what encouragement was there for the stable achievements of architecture? In vain does the architect antic and grimace to conceal his despair; his business is to put on a front. If he is not a Pecksniff at heart, he will at any rate have to serve Mr. Veneering. A guide book of 1826 refers to a Masonic Hall "somewhat in the Gothic style"; and we can characterize all the buildings of the period by saying that they were "somewhat" like architecture—a little more than scenery, a little less than solids.

For a while it seemed as if the Gothic revival might give the prevailing cast to nineteenth-century building; for if this mode was adopted at first because it was picturesque and historic it was later reënforced by the conviction that it was a natural and scientific mode of construction, that it stood for growth and function, as against the arbitrary character of the classic work. The symbols of the organic world were rife in the thought of this period, for in the sphere of thought biology was supplanting physics, and Gothic architecture was supposed peculiarly to be in the line of growth, while that of the Renaissance cut across and, heretically, denied the principle of organic development. Unfortunately

PLATE SIX   *Interior of the New York Crystal Palace.*
            (1853)

the process of disintegration had gone so far that no one current of thought had the power to dominate; and the Gothic style proved to be only the first of a number of discordant influences, derived from industry, from history, from archæology.

Indeed, the chief sign that bears witness to the disintegration of architecture during the formative days of the pioneer is eclecticism; but there is still another—the attempt to justify the industrial process by using solely the materials it had created in abundance. In discussing the plans for the Smithsonian Institution, Robert Dale Owen observed that "of late years a rival material, from the mine, seems encroaching on these [stone, clay, wood] and the next generation may see, arising on our continent, villages, or it may be cities, of iron."

What Owen's generation actually did see, apart from sheet-iron façades and zinc cornices, was the Crystal Palace, which was built in New York in 1853 in imitation of London's exhibition hall of 1850. Ruskin described the original Crystal Palace, with sardonic justice, as a magnified conservatory; and that is about all that can be said for either building. As exercises in technique they doubtless taught many lessons to the iron masters and engineers; but they had scarcely anything to contribute to architecture. A later generation built the train sheds for their smoky railways on this pattern. But the imagination necessary to translate the bare mechanical form into an organic architectural conception did not develop until the eighties—in the great succession that began with Richardson and culminated in Wright.

The growth of eclecticism, on the other hand, had by the middle of the century given the American city the aspect of a museum and the American countryside a touch of the picture-book. Washington Irving's Sunnyside and the first Smithsonian building were in the predominant Gothic mode; but Poe described the mansion of a not altogether imaginary Arnheim as semi-Gothic, semi-Saracenic; and the old Tombs prison in New York got its name from the Egyptian character of its façade. Who can doubt that the design for a *Byzantine* cottage, shown in The American Cottage Builder (1854), was somewhere carried out?

Nettled by the criticism that America was not Europe, the pioneer determined to bring Europe to his doors. Relatively few American architects

PLATE SEVEN   *Byzantine Cottage. (from The American Cottage Builder, 1854)*

during the period, however, had been abroad, and still fewer had been there to any purpose; even men of culture and imagination like Hawthorne and Emerson were not at home in the physical environment of Europe, however intimate they were with its mind. The buildings that were erected under the inspiration of European tours only accentuated the barbarism of the American scene and the poverty of the architect's imagination.

A good part of our architecture today still exhibits the parvenu's uneasiness, and is by turns French, Italian, or more or less obsolete English; but we do not, perhaps, realize with what a difference; for photography and archæological research now make it possible to produce buildings which have all the virtues of the original except originality, whereas the earlier, illiterate development of foreign examples, rehearsed in memory, resulted in a conglomerate form which resembled nothing so much, perhaps, as P. T. Barnum's mermaid.

If the Crystal Palace represents the extreme of industrial art, Colonel Colt's Armsmear represents the opposite—untutored romanticism. Armsmear was built near Hartford, between 1855 and 1862. A writer in the Art Journal for 1876 calls this mansion a "characteristic type of the unique." It was a "long, grand, impressive, contradictory, beautiful, strange thing. . . . An Italian villa in stone, massive, noble, refined, yet not carrying out any decided principles of architecture, it is like the mind of its originator, bold and unusual in its combinations. . . . There is no doubt it is a little Turkish among other things, on one side it has domes, pinnacles, and light, lavish ornamentation, such as Oriental taste delights in. . . . Yet, although the villa is Italian and cosmopolitan, the feeling is English. It is an English home in its substantiality, its home-like and comfortable aspects."

It is, alas! impossible to illustrate in these pages this remarkable specimen of American architecture; but in a lecture on the Present and Future Prospects of Chicago (1846), I have discovered its exact literary equivalent, and it will sum up the crudity and cultural wistfulness of the period perhaps better than any overt description:

"I thank you [apologizes the lecturer] for the patience you have manifested on this occasion, and promise never more to offend in like manner, so long. I have now, as Cowper observes—

J. Clarence Davies Collection, Museum of the City of New York

PLATE EIGHT   *The Tombs, New York's old prison.*

John Haviland, architect. (1838)

The Diaspora of the Pioneer

'Roved for fruit,

Roved far, and gathered much. . . .'

"And can, I think with Scott, surely say that—

'To his promise just

Vich-Alpine has discharged his trust.'

"I propose now, gentlemen, to leave you at Carlang-toghford,

'And thou must keep thee with thy sword.'

"Let me say to you on this occasion, as Campbell does on another:

'Wave, Munich! all your banners wave!

And charge with all your chivalry.'

"And should you in the contest fall, remember with old Homer—

'Such honours Ilion to her hero paid,

And peaceful slept the mighty Hector's shade.'

"Allow me now to close in one of Scott's beautiful strains:

'Charge, Chester, charge! On, Stanley, on!

Were the last words of Marmion.' "

That was American architecture between 1820 and the Civil War—a collection of tags, thrown at random against a building. Architectural forms were brought together by a mere juxtaposition of

materials, held in place by neither imagination nor
logic. There are a number of honorable exceptions
to this rule, for architects like Renwick, who designed
St. Patrick's Cathedral, and Upjohn, who built Trinity Church, had a more sincere understanding of the
conventional task; and by any standard of esthetic
decency the old Gothic building of New York University, on Washington Square, was a far finer
structure than the bulky office building that has
taken its place. Nevertheless, this saving remnant
does not alter the character of the great mass of
work, any more than the occasionally excellent cast-
iron balconies, brought over from the London of the
Regency, alter the depressing character of the great
mass of domestic building. In elevation and interior treatment, these ante-bellum buildings were
all what-nots. Souvenirs of architecture, their
forms dimly recall the monuments of the past without in any sense taking their place.

To tell the truth, a pall had fallen over the industrial city: contemporary writers in the 'forties
and 'fifties speak of the filth and smoke, and without
doubt the chocolate brownstone front was introduced as a measure of protective coloration. In
this dingy environment, men turned to nature as a

refuge against the soiled and bedraggled works of man's creation; and as the creeping factory and railroad train removed Nature farther from their doors, the park was introduced as a more convenient means of escape. The congested capitals of Europe had already learnt this lesson; traveled Americans, like William Cullen Bryant, brought it home; and Central Park, planned in 1853, was the first of the great landscape parks to serve as a people's pleasance. Conceived in contrast to the deflowered landscape and the muddled city, the park alone re-created the traditions of civilization—of man naturalized, and therefore at home, of nature humanized, and therefore enriched. And even today our parks are what our cities should be, and are not.

By 1860 the halcyon day of American civilization was over; the spirit had lingered in letters and scholarship, in the work of Parkman and Motley and Emerson and Melville and Thoreau, but the sun had already sunk below the horizon, and what seemed a promise was in reality an afterglow. By the time the Civil War came, architecture had recorded faithfully the social transformation; it was sullen, grim, gauche, unstable. While in almost every age architecture has an independent value to the spirit, so that we can rejoice in Chartres or Winchester even though we have abandoned the Roman faith, in the early industrial period architecture is reduced to a symptom. Romanticism had not restored the past, nor had industrialism made the future more welcome. Architecture wandered between two worlds, "one dead, the other powerless to be born."

Yet in the very crassness and ugliness of industrialism after the Civil War, there was an element of health. The new captains of industry had faith in themselves and in the cause that they served: if they were brutal, they were nevertheless, according to their own lights, honest, or at the very least forthright: proud of their ability to master the new energies that were swiftly opening up the continent. In the raw new town of Chicago, that transcontinental railroad junction, once a wilderness of **railroad** yards, they encouraged their architects and engineers to fashion the new warehouses and skyscrapers out of the materials of the day, in forms appropriate to the plain utilitarian functions they served. That pioneer spirit resulted in the birth of an architecture that had integrity and self-respect.

PLATE NINE *Central Park, New York. Plan by*
Olmsted and Vaux. (1853)

CHAPTER FIVE

THE DEFEAT OF ROMANTICISM

BETWEEN 1860 and 1890, some of the forces that were latent in industrialism were realized in American architecture. Where the first pioneers had fared timidly, hampered by insufficient resources, the generation that had been stimulated by war industries and profiteering, by the discovery of petroleum and natural gas, by the spanning of the American continent and by cable communication with Europe, rioted over its new-found wealth.

"The Song of the Broad-Ax" still faintly lingered on the Pacific slopes; but the land pioneer was rapidly giving way to the pioneer in industry; and for perhaps the first time during the century, the surplus of capital outran the immediate demand for new plant and equipment. The Iron Age reached its peak of achievement in a series of great bridges, beginning with the Eads Bridge at St. Louis; and romanticism made a last stand. It will pay us, perhaps, to take one last look at the romantic effort, in order to see how impossible and hopeless was the task it set out to perform.

In England, the romantic movement in architecture had made the return to the Middle Ages a definite symbol of social reform: in Ruskin's mind it was associated with the restoration of a medieval type of polity, something like a reformed manor, while with Morris it meant cutting loose from the machine and returning to the meticulous handicraft of the town-guilds. In America, the romantic movement lacked these social and economic implications; and while it is not unfair to say that the literary expression of English romanticism was on the whole much better than the architecture, in the proportion that The Stones of Venice was better than the Ashmolean Museum or the Albert Memorial, the reverse is true on this side of the Atlantic.

Inarticulate as H. H. Richardson, the chief exponent of American romanticism, was, it seemed for a while as if he might breast the tide of mechanical industry and create for a good part of the scene a sense of stability and harmony which it had all too plainly lacked. In relation to his age, however, Richardson was in the biological sense a "sport"; surrounded by jerry-builders, who had degraded the craft of building, and engineers who ignored it, he was perhaps the last of the great medieval line of master-masons.

Richardson began his career in America directly after the Civil War. Almost the first of the new generation of Americans to be trained by the Ecole des Beaux Arts, he brought back to America none of those atrocious adaptations of the French Renaissance like the New York, Philadelphia, and Boston Post Offices. On the contrary, he had come under the influence of Viollet-le-Duc; and for about ten years he struggled with incongruous forms and materials in the anomalous manner known as Free Gothic. The end of this period of experiment came in 1872, when he received the commission for Trinity Church in Boston; and although it was not until ten years later that he saw any Romanesque buildings other than in photographs—for he had not traveled during his student-years in Paris—it was in this sturdy mode that he cast his best work. Richardson was not a decorator, but a builder: in going back to Romanesque precedent, with its round arches and massive stone members, he was following out a dictum of Viollet-le-Duc's: "only primitive sources supply the energy for a long career." Turning away from "applied Gothic," Richardson started to build from the bottom up. So far had the art of masonry disappeared that in Trinity Church Richardson sometimes introduced struts and girders without any attempt to assimilate them in the composition; but as far as any single man could absorb and live with a vanished tradition, Richardson did.

The proof of Richardson's genius as a builder lies in the difference between the accepted drawings for Trinity Church and the finished building. His ideas altered with the progress of the work, and in almost every case the building itself is a vast improvement over the paper design. Moreover, in his capacity as master-mason, Richardson trained an able corps of craftsmen; and so pervasive was his influence that one still finds on houses Richardson never saw, the touches of delicate, leafy stone-carving he had introduced. With carving and sculpture, the other arts entered, and by his fine designs and exacting standards of work, Richardson elevated the position of the minor crafts, at the same time that he turned over unreservedly to men like John La Farge and Augustus St. Gaudens the major elements of decoration.

Probably most people who know Richardson's

Courtesy Ware Library, Columbia University

PLATE TEN   Trinity Church, Boston. Henry Hobson
Richardson, architect. (1873-77)

name vaguely associate him with ecclesiastical work; but Richardson's brand of romanticism was a genuine attempt to embrace the age, and in his long list of public works there are but five churches. If the Pittsburgh Court House and Trinity Church stand out as the hugest of his architectural conceptions, it is the smaller buildings that test the skill and imagination of the master, and the public libraries at North Easton, Malden, and Quincy, Mass., and some of the little railway stations in Massachusetts stand on an equally high level. Richardson pitted his own single powers against the barbarism of the Gilded Age; but, unlike his contemporaries in England, he did not turn his back upon the excellences of industrialism. "The things I want most to design," he said to his biographer, "are a grain-elevator and the interior of a great river-steamboat."

In short, Richardson sought to dominate his age. So nearly did he succeed that in a symposium on the ten finest buildings in America, conducted by an architectural journal in the 'eighties, Richardson was given five. This was no easy victory, and, to tell the truth, it was only a partial one. The case of the State Capitol at Albany, which Richardson and Eidlitz took in hand in 1878, after five million dollars had been squandered on it in the course of ten years' misconstruction, scarcely caricatures the conditions under which the arts struggled to exist. Begun in the style of the Roman Renaissance, the building under Richardson's impetuous touch began to take on Romanesque proportions, only to be legislated back into Renaissance by the offended law-givers!

William Morris Hunt, then at the height of his powers, was commissioned to paint two large mural compositions for the assembly chamber of this blessed building. So much time had been spent in mismanaging the structure that Hunt was given only two months to transfer his cartouche to the panels; but he worked heroically, and, as one of his biographers says, the work was a great triumph. Great, perhaps—but temporary! "The building had fallen into the hands of a political ring, and the poor construction was revealed in the leaking of the massive roof and the settling of the whole structure. Before ten years had passed, great portions of Hunt's paintings flaked off, and what remained was walled up behind the rebuilding necessary to avert utter ruin." In a period like this,

Richardson's comparative success takes on heroic proportions.

II

With the little eddies of eclecticism, with the rage for the Mansard roof, or the introduction of German Gothic, and, a little later, the taste for Queen Anne domesticity, there is scarcely any need to deal; they represented only the dispersion of taste and the collapse of judgment which marked the Gilded Age.

Up to the time of the Chicago World's Fair, Richardson had imitators, and they were not always mean ones. L. H. Buffington, in Minneapolis, had to his credit a number of buildings which would not, perhaps, have dishonored the master himself; but, as so often happens, the tags in Richardson's work were easier to imitate than his spirit and inventiveness; and the chief marks of the style he created are the all-too-solid courses of rough stone, the round arch, the squat columns, and the contrasts in color between the light granite and the dark sandstone or serpentine. Mr. Montgomery Schuyler, an excellent architectural critic, once said, not without reason, that Richardson's houses were not defensible except in a military sense; but one is tempted to read

into these ponderous forms partly the architect's
unconscious desire to combat the infirmity and jerry-
building of his lower contemporaries, and partly his
patron's anxiety to have a seat of refuge against the
uneasy proletariat. A new feudalism was entrench-
ing itself behind the stockades of Homestead and
the other steel-towns of the Pittsburgh district.
Here was a mode of building, solid, formidable, at
times almost brutal, that served the esthetic needs
of the barons of coal and steel almost as well as
the classic met those heroes who had survived the
War of Independence.

I have emphasized what was strong and fine in
Richardson's work in order to show how free it was
from the minor faults of romanticism; and yet it
reckoned without its host, and Richardson, alas!
left scarcely a trace upon the period that followed.
Romanticism was welcomed when it built churches;
tolerated when it built libraries; petted when it built
fine houses; but it could not go much farther.
Richardson was a mason, and masonry was being
driven out by steel; he was an original artist, and
original art was being thrust into the background by
connoisseurship and collection; he was a builder, and
architecture was committing itself more and more

PLATE ELEVEN *Stoughton House, Brattle Street, Cambridge, Mass. Henry Hobson Richardson, architect.*

to the paper plan; he insisted upon building four-square, and building was doomed more and more to *façaderie*. The very strength of Richardson's build-ings was a fatal weakness in the growing centers of commerce and industry. It takes more than a little audacity to tear down one of Richardson's monu-ments, and so, rather ironically, they have held their own against the insurrections of traffic and realty speculation; but the difficulty of getting rid of these Romanesque structures only increased the demand for a more frail and facile method of construc-tion.

Romanticism met its great defeat in the office-building. By the use of the passenger elevator, first designed for an exhibition-tower adjacent to the Crystal Palace in 1853, it had become possible to raise the height of buildings to seven stories: the desire for ground-rents presently increased the height to ten. Beyond this, mere masonry could not go without thickening the supporting piers to such an extent that on a twenty-foot lot more than a quarter of the width would be lost on the lower floors. Richardson's Marshall Field Building in Chicago was seven stories high; and that was about as far as solid stone or brick could climb without becoming undignified and futile by its bulk. The possibilities of masonry and the possibilities of commercial gain through ground-rents were at loggerheads, and by 1888 masonry was defeated.

Richardson, fortunately, did not live to see the undermining of the tradition he had founded and almost established. Within a decade of his death, however, only the empty forms of architecture remained, for the steel-cage of the engineer had become the new structural reality. By 1890 the ground-landlord had discovered, in the language of the pioneer's favorite game, that "the roof's the limit." If that was so, why limit the roof? With this canny perception the skyscraper sprang into being.

During this Gilded Age the standard of the best building had risen almost as high as it had been in America in any earlier period; but the mass of good building had relatively decreased; and the domestic dwellings in both city and country lost those final touches of craftsmanship that had lingered, here and there, up to the Civil War. In the awkward country villas that began to fill the still-remote suburbs of the larger cities, all sense of style and proportion were lost: the plan was marked by meaningless irregularities; a dingy, muddy color spread over the wooden façades. There exists a huge and beautifully printed volume, of which, I believe, there are not more than a hundred copies, on the villas of Newport in 1876: the compiler thereof sought to satisfy the vanity of the original owners and the curiosity of a later generation; yet mid all these examples of the "novel" and the "unique," there is not a single mansion that would satisfy any conceivable line of descendants.

If the level of architecture was low in the country, it touched the bottom of the abyss in the city. As early as 1835 the multiple-family tenement had been introduced in New York as a means of producing congestion, raising the ground-rents, and satisfying in the worst possible way the need of the new immigrants for housing. The conditions of life in these tenements were infinitely lower than they had been in the most primitive farmhouse of the colonial period; their lack of light, lack of water, lack of sanitary facilities, and lack of privacy, created an admirable milieu for the propagation of vice and disease, and their existence in a period which was boasting loudly of the advance of science and industrialism shows, to say the least, how the

myths which inspired the age stood between the eye
and reality, and obscured the actual state of the
modern industrial community.

To the disgrace of the architectural profession
in America, the worst features of tenement-house
construction were standardized in the so-called
dumb-bell tenement which won the first prize in the
model tenement-house competition of 1879; and the
tenements which were designed after this pattern
in the succeeding years combined a maximum lack
of privacy with a minimum of light and air. The
gridiron street-design, the narrow frontage, the deep
lot, all conspired to make good housing difficult in
the larger cities: within this framework good house-
design, indeed, still is difficult. The dumb-bell tenement of the Gilded Age, however, raised bad housing into an art; and the acquisition of this art
in its later developments is now one of the stig-
mata of "progress" in a modern American city. I
say this without irony; the matter is too grave for
jest.

During these same 'seventies, the benefits of poor
housing were extended in New York to those with
money enough to afford something better: the Paris
flat was introduced. The legitimate excuse for the

No. 10.—First prize plan
-- model house compe-
tition of March, 1879,
awarded to James E.
Ware, architect.

No. 11.— Mr. Ware's modi-
fication of his prize plan.

PLATE TWELVE   *The so-called "dumb-bell"*
apartments. (1879)

small apartment was the difficulty of obtaining household service, and the futility of keeping up large houses for small families: this, however, had nothing to do with the actual form that the apartment took, for, apart from the desire for congestion-rents, it is as easy to build apartments for two families as for twenty. The flat is a genuine convenience for the well-to-do visitor to a city; it gives him the atmosphere of a home without many of its major complications, and those who got the taste for this life in Paris were not altogether absurd in desiring to enjoy the same benefits in New York. Unfortunately, what suits a visitor does not necessarily meet the demands of a permanent resident: one may tolerate a blank wall for a week or a month without being depressed, particularly since a good part of a visitor's time is spent outside his home; but to live year after year facing a blank wall or an equally-frowning façade opposite is to be condemned to the environment of a penitentiary.

The result of building apartments in New York and elsewhere was not cheaper rents for smaller quarters: it was smaller quarters without the cheap rents. Those who wanted sunlight and a pleasant view paid a premium for it; those who did not get either paid more than enough for what they got. The result of building apartments which would satisfy only a visitor was to make every family visitors: before the acute housing shortage, yearly removals to new premises were the only palliative that made their occupancy tolerable. The amount of wear and tear and waste, the loss of energy and money and good spirits, produced by the inability of the architect to design adequately under the pecuniary standards of the Gilded Age was colossal. The urban nomad in his own way was as great a spendthrift as the pioneer of the prairie. Both of them had been unable to create a permanent civilization; and both of them paid the price for it.

III

During the first period of pioneering, mechanical improvements had affected the milieu of architecture, but not architecture itself, if one overlooks such ingenuities as the circular and octagon houses of the eighteen-thirties. Slowly, the actual methods of construction changed: the carpenter-builder, who had once performed every operation, gave way to the joiner, whose work profited by putty and paint,

PLATE THIRTEEN   *Slum street in New York.*

curtains and carpets—to the plasterer, who covered up the raw imperfect frame—and to the plumber. Weird ornamental forms for doors and window-architraves, for moldings and pendants, were supplied to the builder by the catalogs of the planing and scroll-saw mills. Invention produced novelties of contortion in wood, unique in ugliness and imbecile in design. Like the zinc and iron statues that graced the buildings of the Centennial Exposition, these devices record the absorption of art in a vain technology.

One need not dwell upon the results of all these miserable efforts, conceived in haste and aborted for profit: the phenomenon was common to industrial civilization at this period, and can be observed in Battersea and Manchester as well as in New York and Pittsburgh. Mr. Thomas Hardy, who was trained as an architect, wrote the esthetic apology for industrialism; and in proclaiming the rightness of our architectural deserts, one cannot help thinking that he transferred to the Wessex countryside a little of the horrible depression he must have acquired in London.

"Gay prospects," exclaimed Mr. Hardy, "wed happily with gay times; but, alas! if the times be not gay! Men have more often suffered from the mockery of a place too smiling than from the oppression of surroundings oversadly tinged. . . . Indeed, it is a question if the exclusive reign of orthodox beauty is not approaching its last quarter. The new vale in Tempe may be a gaunt waste in Thule: human souls may find themselves in closer harmony with external things wearing a somberness distasteful to our race when it was young. Shall we say that man has grown so accustomed to his spiritual Bastille that he no longer looks forward to, and even shrinks from, a casual emergence into unusual brightness?"

Even the best work of the period is blighted with this sombreness: the fact that so many of Richardson's buildings have the heavy air of a prison shows us that the Gilded Age was not, indeed, gay, and that a spiritual Black Friday perpetually threatened the calendar of its days.

IV

If the romantic movement in America proved that the architect could capture only a small part of the field, and go no further than the interests of priv-

PLATE FOURTEEN   *Housing for the Lawrence Manu-
facturing Company. Lowell, Mass.
(Early 1830's)*

ilege allowed, the building of the Brooklyn Bridge showed how well industrialism could handle its problems when its purposes were not limited by the necessity for sloppy workmanship and quick turnover. The story of its building is a tribute to both science and humanity. When John Roebling, the designer of the bridge, died in the midst of his job, the business of construction was taken up by his son, and by his devotion to his task in season and out of season, Washington Roebling became an invalid. Confined to his house on Columbia Heights, for ten years the younger Roebling watched the work through a telescope, and directed it as a general would direct a battle. So goes the legend: it runs rather higher than the tales of mean prudence or mechanical skill which glorified Mr. Samuel Smiles' heroes.

The bridge itself was a testimony to the swift progress of physical science. The strong lines of the bridge, and the beautiful curve described by its suspended cables, were derived from an elegant formula in mathematical physics—the elastic curve. If the architectural elements of the massive piers have perhaps too much the bare quality of engineering, if the pointed arches meet esthetic betrayal in the flat solidity of the cornices, if, in short, the masonry does not sing as Richardson alone perhaps could have made it sing, the steel work itself makes up for this, by the architectural beauty of its pattern; so that beyond any other aspect of New York, I think, the Brooklyn Bridge has been a source of joy and inspiration to the artist. In the later bridges the spanning members are sturdier and the supporting piers and cables are lighter and less essential; and they suffer esthetically by the very ease of their triumph over the difficulties of engineering.

All that the age had just cause for pride in—its advances in science, its skill in handling iron, its personal heroism in the face of dangerous industrial processes, its willingness to attempt the untried and the impossible—came to a head in the Brooklyn Bridge. What was grotesque and barbarous in industrialism was sloughed off in the great bridges. These avenues of communication are, paradoxically, the only enduring monuments that witness a period of uneasy industrial transition; and to this day they communicate a feeling of dignity, stability, and unwavering poise.

The Brooklyn Bridge was opened in 1884; Rich-

Museum of the City of New York

PLATE FIFTEEN   *Brooklyn Bridge. John and
Washington Roebling, engineers (ca. 1883)*

ardson died, after finishing the Pittsburgh Court House, in 1886. There was a short period during which the echoes of Richardson's style resounded in the work of the Western architects; and then in New York two of Richardson's own pupils, Messrs. McKim and White, who had caught the spirit of the period that was to follow the passing of the frontier, prepared an appropriate mold for its activities. By far the finest things in the late 'eighties are the shingled houses which Richardson and Stanford White and a few others developed for seaboard estates: they recovered the spirit of the early vernacular work, and continued the colonial tradition without even faintly recalling colonial forms. This new note, however, was scarcely sounded before it died out; and in the twenty years that followed the conflict between industrialism and romanticism was swallowed up and finally forgotten in the rise of a new mode. Richardson had not died too soon. The quality of mind and culture which shines through his work was opposed to nearly every manifestation of the period that succeeded him.

From this time on, romanticism retained a place for itself only by forfeiting its claims to occupy the whole province of architecture. In churches and college halls where the traditional tie with the Middle Ages had never perhaps been completely broken, its triumphs have been genuine; but although Mr. J. G. Rogers' Harkness Memorial at Yale, or Messrs. Goodhue and Cram's St. Thomas' Church, for example, are admirable architectural showpieces, they have established no precedent for the hundred other kinds of building which the modern community requires; and it is not without significance that in his most recent efforts Mr. Goodhue, for one, had abandoned the molds of romanticism. Unlike Richardson, the surviving romanticists now demand a certain insulation from the modern world; the more intelligent exponents of the movement believe with Dr. Ralph Adams Cram that there is no hope for its achievement throughout the community without a return to "Walled Towns."

Such a retreat is the equivalent of surrender. To hold to Gothic precedent in the hope of re-creating the medieval community is to hope that an ancient bottle will turn potassium permanganate into claret. The romanticists have never fully faced the social and economic problems that attend their architectural solutions: the result is that they have been dependent upon assistance from the very forces and

Museum of the City of New York

PLATE SIXTEEN   *St. Patrick's Cathedral. New York.*

James Renwick, architect.

(1858-79)

institutions which, fundamentally, they aim to combat. Isolated on little islands, secure for the moment, romanticism must view the work on the mainland with a gesture of irate despair; and the only future it dares to face lies behind it!

So much for the weaknesses of romanticism. But there was in the romantic movement, from its beginning in Rousseau, an element of energy and vitality that could not be denied: the belief in nature, as a resource of the human spirit, and a confidence in man's own fountain of vitality, in his organic feelings, his social needs, his sexual urges. What was durable in romanticism was expressed, after Richardson, by his great continuator, Louis Sullivan, who played even more freely with the wavy forms of Richardson's ornament and who affirmed in eloquent, prophetic words what Richardson had only begun to demonstrate in deeds: his faith in democracy and the industrial process. In Frank Lloyd Wright, Sullivan's greater pupil, the respect for nature and the insistence upon the claims of the person were united, even more integrally, with the new order and facility of the machine. These men avoided the pitfalls of romantic archaiscism and historicism, and, along with John

Sticks and Stones

Wellborn Root, laid the foundation for a truly organic architecture, capable of meeting every practical
need and sustaining every ideal claim of the human
spirit.

CHAPTER SIX

THE IMPERIAL FACADE

THE decade between 1890 and 1900 saw the rise of a new period in American architecture. This period had, it is true, been dimly foreshadowed by the grandiose L'Enfant, but if the superficial forms resembled those of the early republic, and if the precedents of classic architecture again became a guide, the dawning age was neither a revival nor a continuation.

In the meanwhile, fresh influences had entered. The generation of students who had studied in the Ecole des Beaux Arts after the Civil War was ready, at last, to follow the lone trail which Richard H. Hunt had blazed. Richardson's most intimate disciples reacted against the stamp of his personality and sought a more neutral mode of expression, consecrated by established canons of good taste. On top of this, the introduction of steel-cage construction removed the necessity for solid masonry, and placed a premium upon the mask. The stage was set for a new act of the drama.

All these influences shaped the style of our architecture when it arose; but the condition that gave it a substantial base was the rise of a new order in America's economic life. Up to this time, the chief industrial problem had been to improve the processes of mechanical production and to stake out new areas for exploitation. One may compare these economic advances to the separate sorties of an army operating on a wide front: any lone adventurer might take his courage in his hands and exploit an invention, or sink an oil well, if he could find it. By 1890 the frontier had closed; the major resources of the country were under the control of the monopolist; it became more important to consolidate gains than freshly to achieve them. Separate lines of railroads were welded into systems; separate steel plants and oil plants were wrought into trusts; and where monopoly did not rest upon a foundation of natural advantage, the "gentleman's agreement" began its service as a useful substitute. The popular movements which sought to challenge the forces of this new regime—the labor movement, socialism, populism—had neither analyzed the situation with sufficient care nor attracted the adherence of the majority. The defeat of Henry George as a local political candidate was symbolic: by 1888 a humane thinker like Edward Bellamy had already accepted the defeat, had embraced the idea of the trust, and had conceived a comprehensive utopia on the basis of letting the process of monopoly go the limit, so that finally, by a mere yank of the levers, the vast economic organizations of the country would become the "property" of the people.

The drift to the open lands came to a full pause. The land-empire had been conquered, and its overlords were waxing in power and riches: the name "millionaire" became the patent of America's new nobility. With the shift from industry to finance went a shift from the producing towns to the spending towns: architecture came to dwell in the stock exchanges, the banks, the shops, and the clubs of the metropolis; if it sought the countryside at all, it established itself in the villas that were newly laid out on hill and shore in the neighborhood of the great cities. The keys to this period are opulence and magnitude: "money to burn."

These years witnessed what the Roman historian, Ferrero, has called a *"véritable recommencement d'histoire."* In the new centers of privilege there arose a scale of living and a mode of architecture which, with all its attendant miseries, depletions, and exploitations, recalled the Rome of the first and second centuries after Christ. It is needless to say that vast acres of buildings, factories, shops, homes, were erected which had no relation at all to the imperial regime; for not everyone participated in either the benefits or the depressions that attended the growth of monopoly; but the accent of this period, the dominant note, was an imperial one. While the commonplace building of the time cannot be ignored, it remains, so to say, out of the picture.

II

Hardly had the process of concentration and consolidation begun before the proper form manifested itself. The occasion for its appearance was the World's Columbian Exposition, opened in 1893. In creating this fair, the enterprise and capacity for organization which the architects of Chicago had applied to the construction of the skyscraper transformed the unkempt wilderness of Jackson Park into the Great White City in the space of two short years. Here the architects of the country, particularly of New York and Chicago, appeared for the first time as a united profession, or, to speak more accurately, as a college. Led by the New Yorkers, who had come more decisively under European influence, they brought to this exposition the combination of skill and taste in all the departments of the work that had, two centuries earlier, created the magnificent formalities of Versailles. There was unity of plan in the grouping of the main buildings about the lagoon; there was unity of tone and color in the gleaming white façades; there was unity of effect in the use of classic orders and classic forms of decoration. Lacking any genuine unity of ideas and purposes—for Root had initially conceived of a variegated oriental setting—the architects of the exposition had achieved the effects of unity by subordinating their work to an established precedent. They chanted a Roman litany above the Babel of individual styles. It was a capital triumph of the academic imagination. If these main buildings were architecture, America had never seen so much of it at one time before. Even that belated Greco-Puritan, Mr. Charles Eliot Norton, was warm in praise.

It would be foolish to quarrel with the style that was chosen for these exposition buildings, or to deny its propriety. Messrs. McKim, White, Hunt, and Burnham divined that they were fated to serve Renaissance despots and emperors with more than Roman power, and unerringly they chose the proper form for their activities. Whereas Rome had cast its spell over the architects of the early Renaissance because they wished once more to enter into its life, the life of its sages and poets and artists, it attracted the architects of the White City because of its external features—because of its stereotyped canons and rules—because of the relatively small number of choices it offered for a lapse in taste—because of its skill in conspicuous waste, and because of that very noncommittal quality in its massive forms which permitted the basilica to become a church, or the temple to become a modern bank.

Of all the Renaissance architects, their impulses and interests were nearest, perhaps, to Robert Adam, whose church at West Wycombe could be turned into a ballroom by the simple act of removing the pews, and permitting the gay walls and decorations to speak for themselves. Behind the white staff façade of the World's Fair buildings was the steel and glass structure of the engineer: the building spoke one language and the "architecture" another. If the coming of the skyscraper had turned masonry into veneer, here was a mode of architecture which was little but veneer.

In their place, at the Fair, these classic buildings were all that could be demanded: Mr. Geoffrey Scott's defense of the Baroque, in The Architecture of Humanism, applies particularly to its essential manifestations in the Garden and the Theater—and why not in the Fair? Form and function, ornament and design, have no inherent relation, one with the other, when the mood of the architect is merely playful: there is no use in discussing the anatomy of architecture when its only aim is fancy dress. As a mask, as a caprice, the classic orders are as justifiable as the icing on a birthday cake: they divert the eye without damaging the structure that they conceal. Unfortunately, the architecture of the Renaissance has a tendency to imitate the haughty queen who advised the commons to eat cake. Logically, it demands that a Wall Street clerk shall live like a Lombardy prince, that a factory should be subordinated to esthetic contemplation; and since these things are impossible, it permits "mere building" to become illiterate and vulgar below the standards of the most debased vernacular. Correct in proportion, elegant in detail, courteous in relation to each other, the buildings of the World's Fair were, nevertheless, only the simulacra of a living architecture: they were the concentrated expression of an age which sought to produce "values" rather than goods. In comparison with this new style, the romanticism of the Victorian Age, with its avid respect for the medieval building traditions, was honesty and dignity itself.

The Roman precedent, modified by the work of Louis XIV and Napoleon III, by Le Nôtre and Haussmann, formed the basis not merely for the World's Fair, but for the host of city plans that were produced in the two decades that followed. It seemed for a while as if the architect might take the place of the engineer as city planner, and that the mangled regularity of the engineer's gridiron plan, laid down without respect to topographic advantage or to use, might be definitely supplanted in the remodeled central districts and in the new extensions and suburbs of the American city. The evil of the World's Fair triumph was that it suggested to the civic enthusiast that every city might become a fair: it introduced the notion of the City Beautiful as a

sort of municipal cosmetic, and reduced the work
of the architect to that of putting a pleasing front
upon the scrappy building, upon the monotonous
streets and the mean houses, that characterized vast
areas in the newer and larger cities.

If the engineer who had devoted himself to sewers
and street-plans alone had been superficial, the architectural city planner who centered attention upon
parkways alone, grand avenues alone, and plazas
like the Place de l'Etoile alone, was equally superficial. The civic center and the parkway represented
the better and more constructive side of this effort:
in Cleveland, in Pittsburgh, in Springfield, Mass.,
harmonious groups of white buildings raised their
heads above the tangle of commercial traffic, and in
the restoration of L'Enfant's plan for Washington,
the realities of the imperial regime at length caught
up with the dreamer born out of his due time. A
good many of these plans, however, were patheti-
cally immature. One of the reports for Manhattan, for example, devoted pages and pages to
showing the improvement that would follow the
demolition of the wall around Central Park—and
the importance of clipped trees in the design of
grand avenues!

Plainly, the architect did not face with sufficient realism the colossal task with which he was confronted in the renovation of the city. He accepted his improvements too much at the value placed upon them by the leaders of Big Business—as a creator of land-values, as an element in increasing the commercial attractiveness of the city. Did not Mr. Daniel Burnham himself point to the improvements in Periclean Athens, not as the embodiment of Athenian citizenship and religion at its highest point, but as a measure for increasing the attractiveness of the city to visitors from abroad? Cut off from his true function to serve and beautify the community, made an accessory of business itself, like the merest salesman or advertising agent, it is no wonder that the architect speedily lost his leadership; and that the initiative went once again into the hands of the engineer.

The main merit of all these efforts to perpetuate the World's Fair is that they sought to achieve some of the dignity and decisiveness of the formal plan. Their weakness was that they neglected new elements, like the billboard, the skysign, the subway, the tall building, which undermined the effects of the plan even when it was achieved. In their efforts to escape from the welter of misguided commercial enterprise, the advocates of the city beautiful placed too great reliance upon spots of outward order and decency; they took refuge in the paper symmetry of axial avenues and round-points, as one finds them in Haussmann's Paris, and neglected the deeper and more genuine beauties of, let us say, the High Street in Oxford or Chipping Camden, or of many another European town that had achieved completion in its essentials before the nineteenth century.

In short, the advocates of the city beautiful sought a remedy on paper which could be purchased only by a thorough reorganization of the community's life. If all this applies to the better side of the World's Fair, it touches even more emphatically the worse.

The twenty years between 1890 and 1910 saw the complete rehabilitation of the Roman mode, as the very cloak and costume of imperial enterprise. The main effort of architecture was to give an effect of dignity and permanence to the façades of the principal thoroughfares: the public buildings must dominate the compositions, numerous boulevards and avenues must concentrate the traffic at certain points and guide the stranger to the markets and amusements: where possible, as in the Chicago plan, by Messrs. Burnham and Bennett, avenues must be cut through the gridiron pattern of blocks in order to achieve these effects. If this imperial street system is somewhat arbitrary, and if the necessary work of grading, filling, demolishing, and purchasing existing property rights is extremely costly, the end, nevertheless, justifies the means—the architecture impresses and awes a populace that shares vicariously in it glories. Should the effect prove a little too austere and formidable, the monuments will be offset with circuses and hippodromes.

In all this, the World's Fair was a precise and classic example, for it reproduced in miniature the imperial order. When the panic of 1893 kept people away from the exhibitions of art, industry, and culture, sideshows were promptly introduced by the astute organizers. Beyond the serene classic façades, which recalled the elevation of a Marcus Aurelius, sprawled the barkers, the freaks, and the tricksters, whose gaudy booths might have reminded the spectator of the other side of the imperial shield—the gaminism of Petronius Arbiter. The transforma-

The Imperial Façade

tion of these white façades into the Gay White Ways
came during the next decade; whilst the sideshows
achieved a separate existence as "Coney Island." On
top of this came the development of the mildly glad-
iatorial spectacles of football and baseball: at first
invented for playful exercise, they became a standard
means of exhibition by more or less professional performers. The erection of numerous amphitheaters
and arenas, such as the Yale Bowl, the Harvard
Stadium, the Lewisohn Stadium, and their counter-
parts in the West, rounded out the imperial spectacle.

By a happy congruence of forces, the large-scale
manufacture of Portland cement, and the reintro-
duction of the Roman method of concrete construction, came during the same period. Can anyone
contemplate this scene and still fancy that imperialism was nothing more than a move for foreign
markets and territories of exploitation? On the
contrary, it was a tendency that expressed itself in
every department of Western civilization, and if it
appears most naked, perhaps, in America, that is
only because, as in the earlier periods, there was so
little here to stand in its way. Mr. Louis Sullivan
might well complain, in The Autobiography of an

Idea, that imperialism stifled the more creative modes of architecture which might have derived from our fine achievements in science, from our tentative experiments in democracy. It seems inevitable, however, that the dominant fact in our civilization should stamp the most important monuments and buildings with its image. In justice to the great professors of the classic style, Messrs. McKim and Burnham and Carrere and Hastings, one must admit that the age shaped them and chose them and used them for its ends. Their mode of building was almost unescapably determined by the milieu in which they worked.

The change in the social scene which favored an imperial setting was not without its effects upon the industries that supplied the materials for architecture, and upon the processes of building itself. Financial concentration in the stone quarries, for example, was abetted by the creation of a national system of rail transportation, and partly, perhaps, by the elaboration of the mechanical equipment for cutting and trimming stone beyond a point where a small plant could work economically. The result was that during this period numerous small local quarries, which had been called into existence by Richardson's fine eye for color contrasts, were allowed to lapse. Vermont marble and Indiana limestone served better the traditions that had been created in the White City.

The carrying of coals to Newcastle is always a pathetic practice; it remained for the imperial age to make it a subject for boasting. Just as many Connecticut towns whose nearby fields are full of excellent granite boulders, boast a bank or a library of remote marble, so New York City, which has a solid foundation of schist, gneiss, and limestone, can point to only a handful of buildings, notably the College of the City of New York and Mr. Goodhue's Church of the Intercession, in which these excellent local materials were used. The curious result of being able by means of railway transportation to draw upon the ends of the earth for materials has been, not variety, but monotony. Under the imperial order the architect was forced to design structures that were identical in style, treatment, and material, though they were placed thousands of miles apart and differed in every important function. This ignorance of regional resources is not incompatible with grand effects, or even on occasion with decently good architecture. But it does not profit by that fine adaptation to site, that justness of proportion in the size of window and slope of roof, which is an earnest of the architect's mastery of the local situation. Substitute Manila for the military colony of Timgad, or Los Angeles for Alexandria, and it is plain that we have here another aspect of Ferrero's generalization. Even architects whose place of work was nearer to the site of their buildings were, nevertheless, compelled to copy the style of the more successful practitioners in New York and Chicago.

In government, in industry, in architecture, the imperial age was one. The underlying policy of imperialism is to exploit the life and resources of separate regions for the benefit of the holders of privilege in the capital city. Under this rule, all roads lead literally to Rome. While, as the German historian, W. H. Riehl, points out, the provincial highroads served to bring the city out into the countryside, the railroads served to bring the major cities together and to drain the products of rural regions into the metropolis. It was no accident that the great triumphs of American architecture during the imperial period were the railroad stations; particularly the Pennsylvania and the Grand Central

Museum of the City of New York

PLATE SEVENTEEN *Concourse of Pennsylvania Station, New York, and Train Hall, showing steel construction. McKim, Mead and White, architects.*

The Imperial Façade

in New York, and the Union Station in Washington.
Nor is it by mere chance that the Washington and
the Pennsylvania stations are the monuments to
two architects, McKim and Burnham, who wor-
shiped most whole-heartedly at the imperial shrine.
With capital insight, these men established the
American Academy at Rome: they recognized their
home.

Esthetically considered, it is true, perhaps, that
the finest element in the Pennsylvania station is the
train hall, where the architect has dealt sincerely
with his steel elements and has not permitted himself
to cast a fond, retrospective eye upon the Roman
baths. When all allowances are made, however, there
remains less for criticism in the railway stations and
the stadiums—those genuinely Roman bequests—
than in any of the other imperial monuments. Indeed, so well does Roman architecture lend itself to
the railroad station that one of the prime virtues of
such a building, namely ease of circulation, was even
communicated to the New York Public Library,
where it is nothing but a nuisance, since it both increases the amount of noise and diminishes the
amount of space for reading rooms that are already
overcrowded.

[139]

Here, indeed, is the capital defect of an established and formalized mode: it tends to make the architect think of a new problem in terms of an old solution for a different problem. Mr. Charles McKim, for example, indignantly withdrew from the competition over the New York Public Library because the demands of the librarian for a convenient and expeditious administration of his business interfered with the full-blown conception which Mr. McKim had in mind. All this happened after years of demonstration in the Boston Library of Messrs. McKim and White's failure to meet that problem squarely; and it apparently was not affected by Mr. McKim's experience with the great Columbia Library, which has ample space for everything except books. In short, the classic style served well enough only when the building to be erected had some direct relation to the needs and interests of the Roman world— the concourse of idlers in the baths or the tiers of spectators in the circuses and hippodromes. When it came face to face with our own day, it had but little to say, and it said that badly, as anyone who will patiently examine the superimposed orders on the American Telegraph Building in New York will discover for himself.

The Imperial Façade

III

With the transition from republican to imperial Rome, numerous monuments were erected to the Divine Cæsar. Within a much shorter time than marked the growth of the imperial tradition in America, a similar edification of patriotic memories took place.

In the restoration of the original plan of Washington, which began in 1901, the axis of the plan was so altered as to make it pass through the Washington Monument; and at the same time the place of the Lincoln Memorial, designed by the late Mr. Henry Bacon, a pupil of Mr. McKim's, was assigned. This was the first of a whole series of temples devoted to the national deities. In the Lincoln Memorial, in the McKinley Memorial at Niles, Ohio, in the Hall of Fame at New York University, and in their prototype, Grant's Tomb, one feels not the living beauty of our American past, but the mortuary air of archæology. The America that Lincoln was bred in, the homespun and humane and humorous America that he wished to preserve, has nothing in common with the sedulously classic monument that was erected to his memory. Who lives in that shrine,

I wonder—Lincoln, or the men who conceived it: the leader who beheld the mournful victory of the Civil War, or the generation that took pleasure in the mean triumph of the Spanish-American exploit, and placed the imperial standard in the Philippines and the Caribbean?

On the plane of private citizenship, a similar movement took place: while before 1890 one can count the tombs in our cemeteries that boast loudly of the owner's earthly possessions and power, from that time onward the miniature temple-mausoleum becomes more and more frequent. In fact, an entire history of architecture could be deduced from our cemeteries; all that has so far been described could be marked in the progress from the simple slab, carved in almost Attic purity with a weeping willow or a cubistic cherub, that characterized the eighteenth century, to the bad lettering and the more awkward headstones of the early nineteenth century; and from this to the introduction of polished granite and iron ornament in the post-Civil War cemetery, down to the mechanically perfect mausoleum, where the corpses are packed like the occupants of a subway train, that some of our more effusively progressive communities boast of today. As we live, so we die:

no wonder Shelley described Hell as a place much like London.

The Roman development of New York, Chicago, Washington, and the lesser metropolises, had an important effect upon the homes of the people. Historically, the imperial monument and the slum-tenement go hand in hand. The same process that creates an unearned increment for the landlords who possess favored sites, contributes a generous quota—which might be called the unearned excrement—of depression, overcrowding, and bad living, in the dormitory districts of the city. This had happened in imperial Rome; it had happened again in Paris under Napoleon III, where Haussmann's sweeping reconstructions created new slums in the districts behind the grand avenues, quite as bad, if far less obvious, as those that had been cleared away; and it happened once again in our American cities. Whereas in Rome a certain limit, however, was placed upon the expansion of the city because of the low development of vehicular traffic, the rise of mechanical transportation placed no bounds at all on the American city. If Rome was forced to create huge engineering projects like aqueducts and sewers in order to cleanse the inhabitants and remove the

offal of its congested districts, the American city
followed the example of the modern Romes like London and Paris by devising man-sewers, in which the
mass of plebeians could be daily drained back and
forth between their dormitories and their factories.

So far from relieving congestion, these colossal
pieces of engineering only made more of it possible:
by pouring more feeder lines into the central district
of New York, Boston, Chicago, or where you will,
rapid transit increased the housing congestion at
one end and the business-congestion at the other. As
for the primary sewer system devised for the imperial
metropolis, it could scarcely even claim, with rapid
transit, that it was a valuable commercial investment.
The water outlets of New York are so thoroughly
polluted that not merely have the shad and the
oyster beds vanished from the Hudson River, where
both once flourished, but it is a serious question
whether the tides can continue to transport their
vast load of sewage without a preliminary reduction
of its content. Like the extension of the water con-
duits into the Adirondacks, all these necessary little
improvements add to the per capita cost of living in
an imperial metropolis, without providing a single

benefit that a smaller city with no need for such improvements does not enjoy. In the matter of public parks, for example, the Committee on Congestion in New York, in 1911, calculated that the park space needed for the East Side alone, on the scale provided by the city of Hartford, would be greater than the entire area of Manhattan Island. In short, even for its bare utilitarian requirements, the mass-city, as the Germans call it, costs more and gives less than communities which have not had imperial greatness inflicted upon them.

As to the more positive improvements under the imperial regime, history leaves no doubt as to their dubious character, and current observation only reinforces history's lesson. In discussing the growth of the tenement in Rome after the Great Fire, Friedlander says:

"The motives for piling up storeys were as strong as ever: the site for Cæsar's Forum had cost over £875,000 compensation to tenants and ground landlords. Rome had loftier houses than modern capital. A disproportionately large part of the area available for building was monopolized by the few, in consequence of the waste of space in the plethoric architecture of the day, and a very considerable portion was swallowed up by the public places, such as the imperial forums, which took up six hectares, as well as by the traffic regulations and extensions of the streets. The transformation and decoration of Rome by the Cæsars enhanced the scarcity of housing, as did Napoleon III's improvements in Paris. A further adjutory cause of the increase in the price of dwellings was the habit of speculation in house property (which Crassus had practiced in great style) and the monopoly of the proprietors, in consequence of which houses were let and sublet."

It would be tedious to draw out the parallel: given similar social conditions in America we have not been able to escape the same social results, even down to the fact that the palliatives of private philanthropy flourish here again as they had not flourished anywhere on the same scale since the Roman Empire. So much for imperial greatness. When an architect like Mr. Edward Bennett can say, as he did in The Significance of the Fine Arts: "House the people densely, if necessary, but conserve great areas for recreation," we need not be in doubt as to who will profit by the density and who will profit, at the other end, by the recreation. It is not merely that the park must be produced to remedy the congestion: it is even more that the congestion must be produced in order to provide for the park. To profit by both the disease and the remedy is one of the master-strokes of imperialist enterprise. Mr. Daniel Burnham said of the World's Fair, according to Mr. Bennett and Mr. Charles Moore, "that it is what the Romans would have wished to create in permanent form." One may say of our imperial cities that they are what the Romans did create—but whether the form will be permanent or not is a matter we may leave to the sardonic attentions of history

For my own part, I think we have at last acquired a criterion which will enable us to sum up the architecture of the imperial age, and deal justly with these railroad stations and stadiums, these sewers and circuses, these aqueducts and parkways and grand avenues. Our imperial architecture is an architecture of compensation: it provides grandiloquent stones for people who have been deprived of bread and sunlight and all that keeps man from becoming vile. Behind the monumental façades of our metropolises trudges a landless proletariat, doomed to the servile routine of the factory system;

[147]

and beyond the great cities lies a countryside whose goods are drained away, whose children are uprooted from the soil on the prospect of easy gain and endless amusements, and whose remaining cultivators are steadily drifting into the ranks of an abject tenantry. This is not a casual observation: it is the translation of the last three census reports into plain English. Can one take the pretensions of this architecture seriously; can one worry about its esthetics or take full delight in such finer forms as Mr. Pope's Temple of the Scottish Rite in Washington, or Mr. Bacon's Lincoln Memorial? Yes, perhaps—if one refuses to look beyond the mask.

Even in some of its proudest buildings, the imperial show wears thin; and one need not peer into the slums beyond in order to realize its defects. The rear of the Metropolitan Museum or the Brooklyn Museum, for example, might be the rear of a row of Bronx tenements or Long Island City factories, so gaunt and barren and hideous is their aspect. If the imperial age was foreshadowed in the World's Fair, it has received its apotheosis in the museum. In contrast to the local museums one still finds occasionally in Europe, which are little more than extensions of the local curio cabinet, the imperial museum is essentially a loot-heap, a comprehensive repository for plunder. The sage Viollet-le-Duc once patly said that he preferred to see his apples hanging on a tree, rather than arranged in rows in the fruit shop: but the animus of the museum is to value the plucked fruit more than the tree that bore it.

Into the museum come the disjecta membra of other lands, other cultures, other civilizations. All that had once been a living faith and practice is here reduced to a separate specimen, pattern, or form. For the museum, the world of art has already been created: the future is restricted to a duplication of the perfected past. This animus is identic with that which made the Romans so skillful in copying Greek statues and so dull in carving their own; a desirable habit of humility were it not for the fact that the works of art in the past could not have been created had our ancestors been so punctual in respect to finished designs. The one thing the museum cannot attempt to do is to supply a soil for living art: all that it can present is a pattern for reproduction. To the extent that an insincere or imitative art is better than no art at all, the Imperial Age marked

an advance: to the extent, however, that a living
art is a fresh gesture of the spirit, the museum con-
fessed all too plainly that the age had no fresh
gestures to make; on that score, it was a failure,
and the copying of period furniture and the design
of period architecture were the livid proofs of that
failure

The museum is a manifestation of our curiosity,
our acquisitiveness, our essentially predatory culture; and these qualities were copiously exhibited in
the architecture of imperialism. It would be foolish
to reproach the great run of architects for exploit-
ing the characteristics of their age; for even those
who in belief and design have remained outside the
age—such resolute advocates of a medieval polity as
Dr. Ralph Adams Cram—have not been able to divert
its currents. In so far as we have learned to care
more for empire than for a community of freemen,
living the good life, more for dominion over palm
and pine than for the humane discipline of ourselves,
the architect has but enshrined our desires. The
opulence, the waste of resources and energies, the
perversion of human effort represented in this architecture are but the outcome of our general scheme
of working and living. Architecture, like govern-

ment, is about as good as a community deserves. The shell that we create for ourselves marks our spiritual development as plainly as that of a snail denotes its species. If sometimes architecture becomes frozen music, we have ourselves to thank when it is a pompous blare of meaningless sounds.

CHAPTER SEVEN

THE AGE OF THE MACHINE

SINCE 1910 the momentum of the Imperial Age
seems to have slackened a little: at any rate, in architecture it has lost much of the original energy which
had been given to it by the success of the Chicago
Exposition. It may be, as Henry Adams hinted,
that the rate of change in the modern world has
altered, so that processes which required centuries
for their consummation before the coming of the
dynamo have been accelerated into decades.

With events and buildings so close to us, it is
almost impossible to rate their relative importance;
all that I can do in the present chapter is to single
out one or two of the more important threads which,
it seems to me, are bound to give the predominant
color to the fabric of our architecture. It is fairly
easy to see, however, why the imperial order has
not stamped every aspect of our building: for one
thing, eclecticism has not merely persisted, but the
new familiarity that the American architect has
gained with authentic European and Asiatic work

outside the province of the classic has increased the range of eclecticism. So the baroque architecture of Spain, which flourished so well in Mexico, and the ecclesiastical architecture of Byzantium and Syria, have added a dubious charm to our wardrobe: from the first came new lessons in ornament and color, applied with great success by Mr. Bertram Goodhue in the Panama-Pacific Exposition, and now budding lustily in southern villas and gardens; and from the second the architect is learning the importance of mass and outline—the essentials in monolithic construction.

Apart from this, however, the imperial regime has been stalled by its own weight. The cost of cutting through new streets, widening grand avenues, and in general putting on a monumental front has put the pure architect at a disadvantage: there is the same disparity between his plans and the actual aims of the commercial community as there is, quite often, between the prospectus and the actual organization of an industry. Within the precincts of the modern city, the engineer, whose utilitarian eye has never blinked at the necessity for profitable enterprise, and whose interest in human beings as loads, weights, stresses, or units pays no attention to their qualitative demands as human beings—within these precincts, I say, the engineer has recovered his supremacy.

Here, in fact, is the paradox of American architecture. In our suburban houses we have frequently achieved the excellence of Forest Hills and Bronxville; in our public buildings we tend more easily to approach the strength and originality of Mr. Goodhue's State Capitol for Nebraska; in fact, never before have the individual achievements of American architects been so rich, so varied, and so promising. In that part of architecture which lies outside the purlieus of our commercial system—I mean the prosperous country homes and college buildings and churches and municipal institutions—a tradition of good building and tactful design has been established. At this point, unfortunately, the scope of the architect has become narrowed: the forces that create the great majority of our buildings lie quite outside the cultivated field in which he works. Through the mechanical reorganization of the entire milieu, the place of architecture has become restricted; and even when architecture takes root in some unnoticed crevice, it blooms only to be cut down at the first "business opportunity."

The processes which are inimical to architecture are, perhaps, seen at their worst in the business district of the metropolis; but more and more they tend to spread throughout the rest of the community. Mr. Charles McKim, for example, was enthusiastic over Mr. Burnham's design for the Illinois Trust and Savings Bank in Chicago, and predicted that it would long be a monument to his genius. "But unfortunately," as Mr. Burnham's biographer says, "unfortunately for Mr. McKim's reputation as a prophet, he was unappreciative of the rapid growth of Chicago, the consequent appreciation in the value of real estate in the Loop district, and the expansive force of a great bank. This beautiful building is doomed to be replaced by one which will tower into the air to the permissible height of structures in the business section of Chicago." The alternative to this destruction is an even more ignominious state of preservation; such a state as the Knickerbocker Trust Company building achieved in New York, or the old Customs House in Boston, both of which have been smothered under irrelevant skyscrapers. Even where economic necessity plays no distinct part, the forms of business take precedence over the forms of humanism—as in the Shipping Board's York Village, where as soon as the direction of the community planner was removed a hideous and illiterate row of shop-fronts was erected, instead of that provided by the architect, in spite of the fact that the difference in cost was negligible.

Unfortunately for architecture, every district of the modern city tends to become a business district, in the sense that its development takes place less in response to direct human needs than to the chances and exigencies of sale. It is not merely business buildings that are affected by the inherent instability of enterprises to which profit and rent have become Ideal Ends: the same thing is happening to the great mass of houses and apartments which are designed for sale. Scarcely any element in our architecture and city planning is free from the encroachment, direct or indirect, of business enterprise. The old Boulevard in New York, for example, which was laid out by the Tweed ring long before the land on either side was used for anything but squatters' farms, was almost totally disrupted by the building of the first subways, and it has taken twenty years to effect even a partial recovery. The widening of part of Park Avenue by slicing off its central grass plot has just been accomplished, in order to relieve traffic congestion; and it needs only a little time before underground and overground traffic will cause the gradual reduction of our other parkways—even those which now seem secure.

The task of noting the manifold ways in which our economic system has affected architecture would require an essay by itself: it will be more pertinent here, perhaps, to pay attention to the processes through which our economic system has worked; and in particular to gauge the results of introducing mechanical methods of production, and mechanical forms into provinces which were once wholly occupied by handicraft. The chief influence in eliminating the architect from the great bulk of our building is the machine itself: in blotting out the elements of personality and individual choice it has blotted out the architect, who inherited these qualities from the carpenter-builder. Mr. H. G. Wells, in The New Macchiavelli, described Altiora and Oscar Bailey as having the temperament that would cut down trees and put sanitary glass lamp-shades in their stead; and this animus has gone pretty far in both building and city planning, for the reason that lamp-shades may be manufactured quickly for sale, and trees cannot. It is time, perhaps, that we isolated the machine and examined its workings. What is the basis of our machine-ritual, and what place has it in relation to the good life?

II

Before we discuss the influence of machinery upon building, let us consider the building itself as an architectural whole.

Up to the nineteenth century, a house might be a shelter and a work of art. Once it was erected, it had few internal functions to perform: its physiological system, if we may use a crude and inaccurate metaphor, was of the lowest order. An open fire with a chimney, windows that opened and closed—these were its most lively pretensions. Palladio, in his little book on the Five Orders, actually has suggestions for cooling the hot Italian villa by a system of flues conducted into an underground chamber from which cold air would circulate; but this ingenious scheme was on the plane of Leonardo's flying machine—an imaginative anticipation, I suppose, rather than a project.

With the exception of Wren's suggestions for ventilating the Houses of Parliament, and Sir

Humphrey Davy's actual installation of apparatus for this purpose, it was not until the last quarter of the nineteenth century that engineers turned their minds to this problem, in America. Yankee ingenuity had devised central heating before the Civil War, and one of the first numbers of Harper's Weekly contained an article deploring the excessive warmth of American interiors; and at one time or another during the century, universal running water, open plumbing, gas, electric lighting, drinking fountains, and high speed electric elevators made their way into the design of modern buildings. In Europe these changes came reluctantly, because of the existence of vast numbers of houses that had been built without a mechanical equipment; so that many a student at the Beaux Arts returned from an attic in the Latin quarter where water was carried in pails up to the seventh story, to design houses in which the labor-saving devices became an essential element in the plan. It is only now, however, during the last two decades, that the full effect of these innovations has been felt.

The economic outcome of all these changes can be expressed mathematically; and it is significant. According to an estimate by Mr. Henry Wright in the Journal of the American Institute of Architects, the structure of the dwelling house represented over ninety per cent of the cost in 1800. Throughout the century there was a slow, steady increase in the amount necessary for site, fixtures, and appliances, until, in 1900, the curve takes a sharp upward rise; with the result that in 1920 the cost of site and mechanical equipment has risen to almost one-half the total cost of the house. If these estimates apply to the simple dwelling house, they apply, perhaps, with even greater force to the tenement, the office building, the factory, and the loft: here the cost of ventilation, of fireproof construction, of fire-prevention and fire-escaping devices, makes the engineering equipment bulk even more heavily.

Whereas in the first stages of industrial development the factory affected the environment of architecture, in its latest state the factory has become the environment. A modern building is an establishment devoted to the manufacture of light, the circulation of air, the maintenance of a uniform temperature, and the vertical transportation of its occupants. Judged by the standards of the laboratory, the modern building is, alas! an imperfect machine: the engineers of a certain public service corporation, for example, have discovered that the habit of punching windows in the walls of the building-machine is responsible for great leakages which make difficult the heating and cooling of the plant; and they hold that the maximum efficiency demands the elimination of windows, the provision of "treated" air, and the lighting of the building throughout the day by electricity.

All this would perhaps seem a little fantastic, were it not for the fact that we have step by step approached the reality. Except for our old-fashioned prejudice in favor of windows, which holds over from a time when one could see a green field or a passing neighbor by sitting at one, the transformation favored by the engineers has already been accomplished. Just because of the ease in installing fans, lights, and radiators in a modern building, a good part of the interiors of our skyscrapers are fed day and night with artificial light and ventilation. The margin of misuse under this method of construction is necessarily great; the province of design, limited. Instead of the architect's paying attention to exposure, natural circulation, and direct daylight, and making a layout which will achieve these necessary ends, he is forced to center his efforts on the maximum exploitation of land. Where the natural factors are flouted or neglected, the engineer is always ready to provide a mechanical substitute—"just as good as the original" and much more expensive.

By systematically neglecting the simplest elements of city planning, we have provided a large and profitable field for all the palliative devices of engineering: where we eliminate sunlight we introduce electric light; where we congest business, we build skyscrapers; where we overcrowd the thoroughfares with traffic we burrow subways; where we permit the city to become congested with a population whose density would not be tolerated in a well-designed community, we conduct water hundreds of miles by aqueducts to bathe them and slake their thirst; where we rob them of the faintest trace of vegetation or fresh air, we build metalled roads which will take a small portion of them, once a week, out into the countryside. It is all a very profitable business for the companies that supply light and rapid transit and motor cars, and the rest of it; but the underlying population pays for its improvements both ways—that is, it stands the gratuitous loss, and it pays "through the nose" for the remedy.

These mechanical improvements, these labyrinths

of subways, these audacious towers, these endless miles of asphalted streets, do not represent a triumph of human effort: they stand for its comprehensive misapplication. Where an inventive age follows methods which have no relation to an intelligent and humane existence, an imaginative one would not be caught by the necessity. By turning our environment over to the machine we have robbed the machine of the one promise it held out—that of enabling us to humanize more thoroughly the details of our existence.

III

To return to architecture. A further effect of the machine process on the internal economy of the modern building is that it lends itself to rapid production and quick turnover. This has been very well put by Mr. Bassett Jones, in an article in The American Architect, which is either a hymn of praise to the machine, or a cool parade of its defects, according to the position one may take.

"As the building more and more takes on the character of the machine," says Mr. Jones, "so does its design, construction, and operation become subject to the same rules that govern . . . a locomotive.

The Age of the Machine

Our grandfathers built for succeeding generations. The rate of development was slow, and a building which would satisfy the demands made upon it for a century would necessarily be of a substantial nature. But with us in a single generation even the best we can do with all the data and facilities at our command is out of date almost before it shows signs of appreciable wear. So a building erected today is outclassed tomorrow. The writer well remembers the late Douglas Robinson, when outlining the location and property to be improved by the construction of a building some twenty years ago, ending his directions with the proviso that it must be 'the cheapest thing that will hold together for fifteen years'! When the amortization charges must be based on so short a period as this, and with land taxes constantly increasing, it becomes obvious that construction must be based upon a cubic foot valuation that prohibits the use of any but the cheapest materials and methods. . . . Even the cost of carrying the required capital inactive during the period of production has its effect in speeding up production to the point where every part of the building that, by any ingenuity of man, can be machine-made must be so made."

Since the features that govern the construction of modern buildings are conditioned by external canons of mechanism, purpose and adaptation to need play a small part in the design, and the esthetic element itself enters largely by accident. The plan of the modern building is not fundamental to its treatment; it derives automatically from the methods and materials employed. The skyscraper is inevitably a honeycomb of cubes, draped with a fireproof material: as mechanically conceived, it is readily convertible: the floors are of uniform height and the windows of uniform spacing, and with no great difficulty the hotel becomes an office building, the office building a loft; and I confidently look forward to seeing the tower floors become apartments—indeed this conversion has already taken place on a small scale. Where the need of spanning a great space without using pillars exists, as in a theater or an auditorium, structural steel has given the architect great freedom; and in these departments he has learned to use his material well; for here steel can do economically and esthetically what masonry can do only at an unseemly cost, or not at all.

What is weak in some of our buildings, however, is

PLATE EIGHTEEN *The Woolworth Building. New York. Cass Gilbert, architect. (1913)*

not the employment of certain materials, but the application of a single formula to every problem. In the bare mechanical shell of the modern skyscraper there is precious little place for architectural modulation and detail; the development of the skyscraper has been towards the pure mechanical form. Our first tall buildings were designed for the most part by men who thought in terms of established architectural forms: Burnham and Root's Monadnock Building, in Chicago, which has exerted such a powerful influence over the new school of German architects, was an almost isolated exception; and, significantly enough, it did not employ the steel skeleton! The academic architects compared the skyscraper to a column, with a base, a shaft, and a capital; and they sought to relieve its empty face with an elaborate modeling of surface, like that of the old Flatiron Building. Then the skyscraper was treated as a tower, and its vertical lines were accented by piers which simulated the acrobatic leap of stone construction: the Woolworth Tower and the Bush Tower were both designed in this fashion, and, in spite of numerous defects in detail, they remain with the new Shelton Hotel in New York among the most satisfactory examples of the skyscraper.

Neither column nor buttress has anything to do with the internal construction of the skyscraper; both forms are "false" or "applied." Picking up the precedent of the old Chicago school, the buildings of the machine period have accepted the logic of the draped cube, and the only gestures of traditional architecture that remain are the ornaments that cling to the very highest and the very lowest stories. Those buildings which do not follow this logic for the most part accentuate the clumsy unimaginativeness of the designer: the new Standard Oil building in New York, with its vestigial orders, shows an interesting profile across the harbor almost in spite of itself, but at a closer range will not bear criticism.

An ornamentalist, like Mr. Louis Sullivan, is perhaps at his best against the simple planes of the modern building: but a different order of imagination, an imagination like that of the Norman builders, is powerless in the face of this problem—or it becomes brutal. If modern building has become engineering, modern architecture retains a precarious foothold as ornament, or to put it more frankly, as scene painting. Indeed, what is the bare interior of a modern office or apartment house but a stage, wait-

PLATE NINETEEN *Wainright Building. St. Louis, Mo.*
Dankmar Adler and Louis H.
Sullivan, architects.

ing for the scenery to be shifted, and a new play to
be put on. It is due to this similarity, I believe, that
modern interior decoration has so boldly accepted
the standards and effects of stage-design. A newspaper critic referred to Mr. Norman-Bel Geddes as
having lined the interior of the Century Theater
with a cathedral: well, in the same way, the interior
of a modern skyscraper is lined with a factory, an
office, or a home.

It is not for nothing that almost every detail of
the mechanized building follows a standard pattern
and preserves a studious anonymity. Except for
the short run of the entrance, the original architect
has no part in its interior development. If the architect himself is largely paralyzed by his problem,
what shall we say of the artisans, and of the surviving handicraft workers who still contribute their
quota of effort to the laying of bricks and stones,
to the joining of pipes, to the plastering of ceilings?
Gone are most of their opportunities for the exercise of skilled intelligence, to say nothing of art:
they might as well make paper-boxes or pans for all
the personal stamp they can give to their work.
Bound to follow the architect's design, as the printer
is supposed to follow the author's words, it is no

wonder that they behave like the poor drudge in
the Chicago Exposition who left bare or half-orna-
mented the columns which the architect had not
bothered to duplicate in full in the haste of finishing
his drawing. Is it any wonder, too, that the last
vestige of guild standards is gone: that the politics
of industry, the bargaining for better wages and
fewer hours, concerns them more than their control
over their job and the honor and veracity of their
workmanship? What kind of work can a man put
into "the cheapest building that will last fifteen
years"?

IV

The chief justification for our achievements in mechanical architecture has been brought forth by
those who believe it has provided the basis for a
new style. Unfortunately, the enthusiasts who
have put the esthetic achievements of mechanical
architecture in a niche by themselves, and who
have serenely disregarded all its lapses and failures
and inefficiencies, have centered their attention
mainly upon its weakest feature—the skyscraper.
I cannot help thinking that they have looked in
the wrong place. The economic and social reasons

PLATE TWENTY   *Detail of ornament around show win-*
dows of the Schlesinger and Meyer
Building (now Carson, Pirie, Scott
and Co.). Chicago, Ill.
Louis H. Sullivan, architect.

for regarding the skyscraper as undesirable have
been briefly alluded to; if they needed any further
confirmation, a week's experience of the miseries
of rapid transit would perhaps be sufficient. It
remains to point out that the esthetic reasons are
just as sound.

All the current praise of the skyscraper boils
down to the fact that the more recent buildings have
ceased to be as bad as their prototypes. Granted.
The uneasy hemming and hawing of ornament, which
once agitated the whole façade, has now been reduced to a concentrated gesture; and the zoning
ordinances that have been established in many large
American cities have transformed the older, top-
heavy building into a tower or a pyramid. That
this is something of an advance is beyond dispute; in
New York one need only compare the Fisk Tire
Building with the United States Tire Building, rep-
resenting respectively the later and the earlier work
of the same architects, to see what a virtue can be
made of legal necessity. A great architecture, however, is something to be seen and felt and lived in.
By this criterion most of our pretentious buildings
are rather pathetic.

When one approaches Manhattan Island, for instance, from the Staten Island Ferry or the Brooklyn Bridge, the great towers on the tip of the island sometimes look like the fairy stalagmites of an opened grotto; and from an occasional vantage point on the twentieth floor of an office building one may now and again recapture this impression. But need I point out that one can count on one's fingers the number of buildings in New York or Chicago that one can approach from the street in similar fashion? For the millions who fill the pavements and shuttle back and forth in tubes, the skyscraper as a tall, cloudward building does not exist. Its esthetic features are the entrance, the elevator, and the window-pocked wall; and if there has been any unique efflorescence of a fresh style at these points, I have been unable to discover it.

What our critics have learned to admire in our great buildings is their photographs—and that is another story. In an article chiefly devoted to praise of the skyscraper, in a number of The Arts, the majority of the illustrations were taken from a point that the man in the street never reaches. In short, it is an architecture, not for men, but for angels and aviators!

If buildings are to be experienced directly, and

not through the vicarious agency of the photograph, the skyscraper defeats its own ends; for a city built so that tall buildings could be approached and appreciated would have avenues ten times the width of the present ones; and a city so generously planned would have no need for the sort of building whose sole economic purpose is to make the most of monopoly and congestion. In order to accommodate the office-dwellers in the Chicago Loop, for example, if a minimum of twenty stories were the restriction, the streets would have to be 241 feet wide, according to a calculation of Mr. Raymond Unwin, in the Journal of the American Institute of Architects.

One need not dwell upon the way in which these obdurate, overwhelming masses take away from the little people who walk in their shadows any semblance of dignity as human beings; it is perhaps inevitable that one of the greatest mechanical achievements in a thoroughly dehumanized civilization should, no doubt unconsciously, achieve this very purpose. It is enough to point out that the virtues of the skyscraper are mainly exercises in technique. They have precious little to do with the human arts of seeing, feeling, and living, or with the noble architectural end of making buildings which stimulate and enhance these arts.

A building that one cannot readily see, a building that reduces the passerby to a mere mote, whirled and buffeted by the winds of traffic, a building that has no accommodating grace or perfection in its interior furnishing, beyond its excellent lavatories —in what sense is such a building a great work of architecture, or how can the mere manner of its construction create a great style? One might as well say, with Robert Dale Owen, that the brummagem gothic of the Smithsonian Institution was a return to organic architecture. Consider what painful efforts of interior decoration are necessary before the skyscraper-apartment can recapture the faded perfume of the home. Indeed, it takes no very discerning eye to see that in a short time we shall be back again in interiors belonging to the period of the ottoman and the whatnot, in order to restore a homely sense of comfort and esthetic ease to the eviscerated structure of the modern fireproof apartment. What chiefly distinguishes our modern American work in this department from that of the disreputable 'eighties is that the earlier architects were conscious of their emptiness, and attempted

feverishly to hide it: whereas our moderns do not
regard emptiness as a serious lapse, and are inclined
to boast about it.

There is a sense, of course, in which these modern
colossi express our civilization. It is a romantic
notion, however, to believe that this is an important
or beautiful fact. Our slums express our civilization, too, and our rubbish heaps tell sermons that
our stones conceal. The only expression that really
matters in architecture is that which contributes
in a direct and positive way to the good life: that is
why there is so much beauty to the square foot in
an old New England village, and so little, beyond
mere picturesqueness, in the modern metropolis. A
building stands or falls, even as a pure work of art,
by its just relation to the city around it. Without
a sense of scale—and the skyscraper has destroyed
our sense of scale—the effect of any single building
is nullified.

v

The provinces in which mechanical architecture
has been genuinely successful are those in which
there have been no conventional precedents, and in
which the structure has achieved a sense of absolute

form by following sympathetically the limitations of material and function. Just as the bridge summed up what was best in early industrialism, so the modern subway station, the modern lunch room, the modern factory, and its educational counterpart, the modern school, have often been cast in molds which would make them conspicuous esthetic achievements. In the Aristotelian sense, every purpose contains an inherent form; and it is only natural that a factory or lunchroom or grain elevator, intelligently conceived, should become a structure quite different in every aspect from the precedents that are upheld in the schools.

It would be a piece of brash esthetic bigotry to deny the esthetic values that derive from machinery: the clean surfaces, the hard lines, the calibrated perfection that the machine has made possible carry with them a beauty quite different from that of handicraft—but often it is a beauty. Our new sensitiveness to the forms of useful objects and purely utilitarian structures is an excellent sign; and it is not surprising that this sensitiveness has arisen first among artists. Many of our power-plants are majestic; many of our modern factories are clean and lithe and smart, designed with unerr-

ing logic and skill. Put alongside buildings in which
the architect has glorified his own idiosyncrasy or
pandered to the ritual of conspicuous waste, our
industrial plants at least have honesty and sincerity
and an inner harmony of form and function. There
is nothing peculiar to machine-technology in these
virtues, however, for the modern factory shares them
with the old New England mill, the modern grain
elevator with the Pennsylvania barn, the steamship
with the clipper, and the airplane hangar with the
castle.

The error with regard to these new forms of
building is the attempt to universalize the mere
process or form, instead of attempting to universalize the scientific spirit in which they have been
conceived. The design for a dwelling-house which
ignores everything but the physical necessities of
the occupants is the product of a limited conception
of science which stops short at physics and mechanics,
and neglects biology, psychology, and sociology. If
it was bad esthetics to design steel frames decorated
with iron cornucopias and flowers, it is equally bad
esthetics to design homes as if babies were hatched
from incubators, and as if wheels, rather than love
and hunger, made the world go round. During the

first movement of industrialism it was the pathetic fallacy that crippled and warped the new achievements of technology; today we are beset by the plutonic fallacy, which turns all living things it touches into metal.

In strict justice to our better sort of mechanical architecture, I must point out that the error of the mechanolators is precisely the opposite error to that of the academies. The weakness of conventional architecture in the schools of the nineteenth century was the fact that it applied only to a limited province: we knew what an orthodox palace or post office would be like, and we had even seen their guilty simulacra in tenement-houses and shopfronts; but no one had ever dared to imagine what a Beaux Arts factory would be like; and such approaches to it as the pottery works in Lambeth only made the possibility more dubious. The weakness of our conventional styles of architecture was that they stopped short at a province called building—which meant the province where the ordinary rules of esthetic decency and politeness were completely abandoned, for lack of a precedent.

The modernist is correct in saying that the mass of building ought to speak the same language; it is well for him to attempt to follow Mr. Louis Sullivan, in his search for a "rule so broad as to admit of no exceptions." Where the modernist becomes confused, however, is in regarding the *dictionary* of modern forms, whose crude elements are exhibited in our factories and skyscrapers and grain elevators, as in any sense equivalent for their creative expression. So far our mechanical architecture is a sort of structural Esperanto: it has a vocabulary without a literature, and when it steps beyond the elements of its grammar it can only translate badly into its own tongue the noble poems and epics that the Romans and Greeks and medieval builders left behind them.

The leaders of modernism do not, indeed, make the mistake that some of their admirers have made: Mr. Frank Lloyd Wright's pleasure pavilions and hotels do not resemble either factories or garages or grain elevators: they represent the same tendencies, perhaps, but they do so with respect to an entirely different set of human purposes. In one important characteristic, Mr. Wright's style has turned its back upon the whole world of engineering: whereas the steel cage lends itself to the vertical skyscraper, Mr. Wright's designs are the very products of the prairie, in their low-lying, horizontal lines, in their flat roofs, while at the same time they defy the neutral gray or black or red of the engineering structure by their colors and ornament.

In sum, the best modern work does not merely respect the machine: it respects the people who use it. It is the lesser artists and architects who, unable to control and mold the products of the machine, have glorified it in its nakedness, much as the producer of musical comedies, in a similar mood of helpless adulation, has "glorified" the American girl —as if either the machine or the girl needed it.

It has been a genuine misfortune in America that, as Mr. Sullivan bitterly pointed out in The Autobiography of an Idea, the growth of imperialism burked the development of a consonant modern style. In Europe, particularly in Finland, Germany, and the Netherlands, the best American work has been appreciated and followed up, and as so often happens, exaggerated; so that the esthetic appreciation of the machine has been carried across the Atlantic and back again, very much in the way that Emerson's individualism was transformed by Nietzsche and became the mystic doctrine of the Superman. Some of the results of this movement

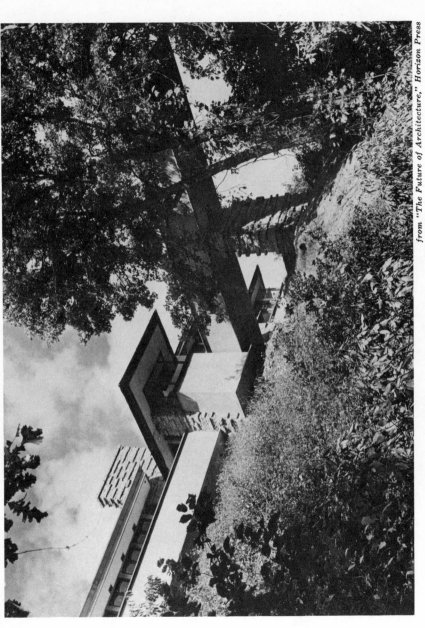

from "The Future of Architecture," Horizon Press

PLATE TWENTY-ONE   Taliesin III. Frank Lloyd Wright's home in Spring Green, Wis. Designed by himself.

are interesting and valid: the work of the Dutch
architects, for example, in the garden suburbs around
Amsterdam: but what pleases one in these new compositions is not the mechanical rigor of form but
the playfulness of spirit—they are good architecture
precisely because they are something more than mere
engineering. Except for a handful of good precedents, our mechanical work in America does not
express this vitality. The machine has stamped us;
and we have not reacted.

Moreover, in the building of separate houses in
the city and its suburbs, where the demands of mechanical efficiency are not so drastic as they are in
the office building, the effect of the machine process
has been to narrow the scope of individual taste and
personality. The designer, whether he is the architect, the owner, or the working contractor, works
within a tradition whose bearing lies beyond him.
Outside this mechanical tradition we have had many
examples of good individual work, like the stone
houses that have been erected around Philadelphia,
and the more or less native cement and adobe houses
in New Mexico and California: but the great mass
of modern houses are no longer framed for some
definite site and some definite occupants: they are

manufactured for a blind market. The boards are cut to length in the sawmill, the roofing is fabricated in a roofing plant, the window frames are cut in standard sizes and put together in the framing factory, the balustrade is done in a turning mill, the very internal fittings like china closets and chests are made in a distant plant, after one of a dozen patterns fixed and exemplified in the catalog. The business of the building worker is reduced to a mere assemblage of parts; and except for the more expensive grades of work, the architect is all but eliminated. The charming designs that the European modernists make testify to the strength of their long architectural tradition even in the face of machinery; the truth is that they fit our modern methods of house-production scarcely much better than the thatched cottage of clay and wattle. The nemesis of mechanism is that it inexorably eliminates the architect—even the architect who worships its achievements!

So much of the detail of a building is established by factory standards and patterns that even the patron himself has precious little scope for giving vent to his impulses in the design or execution of the work; for every divergence from a standardized design represents an additional expense. In fact, the only opportunity for expressing his taste and personality is in choosing the mode in which the house is to be built: he must find his requirements in Italy, Colonial America, France, Tudor England, or Spain—woe to him if he wants to find them in twentieth-century America! Thus the machine process has created a standardized conception of style: of itself it can no more invent a new style than a mummy can beget children. If one wishes a house of red brick it will be Georgian or Colonial; that is to say, the trimming will be white, the woodwork will have classic moldings, and the electric-light fixtures will be pseudo-candlesticks in silvered metal. If one builds a stucco house, one is doomed by similar mechanical canons to rather heavy furniture in the early Renaissance forms, properly duplicated by the furniture makers of Grand Rapids—and so on. The notion of an American stucco house is so foreign to the conception of the machine mode that only the very poor, and the very rich, can afford it. Need I add that Colonial or Italian, when it falls from the mouth of the "realtor" has nothing to do with authentic Colonial or Italian work?

Commercial concentration and the national market

waste resources by neglect, as in the case of the Appalachian forests they squandered them by pillage. Standardized materials and patterns and plans and elevations—here are the ingredients of the architecture of the machine age: by escaping it we get our superficially vivacious suburbs; by accepting it, those vast acres of nondescript monotony that, call them West Philadelphia or Long Island City or what you will, are but the anonymous districts of Coketown. The chief thing needful for the full enjoyment of this architecture is a standardized people. Here our various educational institutions, from the advertising columns of the five-cent magazine to the higher centers of learning, from the movie to the radio, have not perhaps altogether failed the architect.

The manufactured house is set in the midst of a manufactured environment. The quality of this environment calls for satire rather than description; and yet a mere catalog of its details, such as Mr. Sinclair Lewis gave in Babbitt, is almost satire in itself. In this environment the home tends more and more to take last place: Mr. Henry Wright has in fact humorously suggested that at the present increasing ratio of site-costs—roads,

sewers, and so forth—to house-costs, the house itself will disappear in favor of the first item by
1970. The prophetic symbol of this event is the
tendency of the motor-car and the temple-garage
to take precedence over the house. Already these
incubi have begun to occupy the last remaining
patch of space about the suburban house, where up
to a generation ago there was a bit of garden, a
swing for the children, a sandpile, and perhaps a
few fruit trees.

The end of a civilization that considers buildings
as mere machines is that it considers human beings
as mere machine-tenders: it therefore frustrates or
diverts the more vital impulses which would lead to
the culture of the earth or the intelligent care of
the young. Blindly rebellious, men take revenge
upon themselves for their own mistakes: hence the
modern mechanized house, with its luminous bathroom, its elegant furnace, its dainty garbage-dis-
posal system, has become more and more a thing to
get away from. The real excuse for the omnipres-
ent garage is that in a mechanized environment of
subways and house-machines some avenue of escape
and compensation must be left open. Distressing as
a Sunday automobile ride may be on the crowded

highways that lead out of the great city, it is one degree better than remaining in a neighborhood unsuited to permanent human habitation. So intense is the demand for some saving grace, among all these frigid commercial perfections, that handicraft is being patronized once more, in a manner that would have astonished Ruskin, and the more audacious sort of interior decorator is fast restoring the sentimentalities in glass and wax flowers that marked the Victorian Age. This is a pretty comment upon the grand achievements of modern industry and science; but it is better, perhaps, that men should be foolish than that they should be completely dehumanized.

The architecture of other civilizations has sometimes been the brutal emblem of the warrior, like that of the Assyrians: it has remained for the architecture of our own day in America to be fixed and stereotyped and blank, like the mind of a Robot. The age of the machine has produced an architecture fit only for lathes and dynamos to dwell in: incomplete and partial in our applications of science, we have forgotten that there is a science of humanity, as well as a science of material things. Buildings which do not answer to this general description are either aristocratic relics of the age of handicraft, enjoyed only by the rich, or they are fugitive attempts to imitate cheaply the ways and gestures of handicraft.

We have attempted to live off machinery, and the host has devoured us. It is time that we ceased to play the parasite: time that we looked about us, to see what means we have for once more becoming men. The prospects of architecture are not divorced from the prospects of the community. If man is created, as the legends say, in the image of the gods, his buildings are done in the image of his own mind and institutions.

Once our society recovers the initiative again for the human spirit, the machine, instead of being the all-devouring monster, the implacable automaton, that it has actually become in our time, will perform a more useful function in our economy. Though the actual utilization of the machine may diminish, in certain fields, in quantity, the machine will increase in its total significance, since it will be attached to higher human purposes. At this point, all the economies and simplicities the machine has introduced will have a new meaning: we shall take a fresh pleasure in the clarity and order that rationalism first introduced into early renascence architecture and brought to a high pitch of perfection in the machine and its typical products. Because no longer serving as a substitute for life, the machine will at last further life.

CHAPTER EIGHT

ARCHITECTURE AND CIVILIZATION

Iɴ the course of this survey we have seen how architecture and civilization develop hand in hand: the characteristic buildings of each period are the memorials to their dearest institutions. The essential structure of the community—the home, meeting-place, the work-place—remains; but the covering changes and passes, like the civilization itself, when new materials, new methods of work, new ideas and habits and ways of feeling, come into their own.

If this interpretation of the rôle of architecture is just, there is little use in discussing the needs and promises of architecture without relating the shell itself to the informing changes that may or may not take place in the life of the community itself. To fancy that any widespread improvement of architecture lies principally with the architects is an esthetic delusion: in a barren soil the most fertile geniuses are cut off from their full growth. We have not lacked architects of boldness and originality, from Latrobe to Louis H. Sullivan: nor have we lacked men of great ability, from Thomas Jefferson to Bertram Goodhue; nor yet have we lacked men who stood outside the currents of their time and kept their own position, from Richardson to Dr. Cram. With all these capacities at our disposal, our finest efforts in building remain chaotic and undisciplined and dispersed—the reflection of our accumulated civilization.

Our architectural development is bound up with the course of our civilization: this is a truism. To the extent that we permit our institutions and organizations to function blindly, as our bed is made, so must we lie on it; and while we may nevertheless produce isolated buildings of great esthetic interest, like Messrs. Cram and Goodhue's additions to West Point, like The Shelton, like a hundred country estates, the matrix of our physical community will not be affected by the existence of separate jewels; and most of our buildings will not merely be outside the province of the architectural profession—they will be the product of minds untouched, for the most part, by humane standards. Occasionally the accidental result will be good, as has happened sometimes in our skyscrapers and factories and grain elevators; but an architecture that must depend upon accidental results is not exactly a triumph of the imagination, still less is it a triumph of exact technology.

Looking back upon the finished drama, it is convenient to regard our community and our builders as creatures of their environment: once their choices are made, they seem inevitable. On this account even the pomp of the imperial architects can be justified, as the very voice and gesture of the period they consummated. Looking forward, however, this convenient fiction of inevitability is no longer serviceable: we are in the realm of contingency and choice; and at any moment a new factor may be introduced which will alter profoundly the economic and social life of the community. The Great War in Europe, the revolution in Russia, the spread of motor transportation in America, the idea of noncoöperation in India—I select these at random as matters which during the last generation have altered profoundly the unceasing "drift of things."

The future of our civilization depends upon our ability to select and control our heritage from the past, to alter our present attitudes and habits, and to project fresh forms into which our energies may be freely poured. On our ability to re-introduce old elements, as the humanists of the late Middle

Ages brought back the classic literature and un-
covered the Roman monuments, or to introduce new
elements, as the inventors and engineers of the last
century brought in physical science and the ma-
chine-tool technology, our position as creators depends. During the last century our situation has
changed from that of the creators of machinery to
that of creatures of the machine system; and it is
perhaps time that we contrived new elements which
will alter once more the profounder contours of our
civilization.

Unfortunately for our comfort and peace of mind,
any real change in our civilization depends upon
much more complicated, and much more drastic
measures than the old-fashioned reformer, who
sought to work a change of heart or to alter the
distribution of income, ever recognized; and it will
do little good to talk about a "coming renaissance"
unless we have a dim idea of the sort of creature that
is to be born again. Our difficulty, it seems to me,
is due to the fact that the human sciences have
lagged behind the physical ones; and up to the
present time our good intentions have been frus-
trated for the lack of the necessary instruments of
analysis. It may be helpful and amusing, however,

to see what we can do in this department with the instruments that are already at hand.

In every community, as Frédéric Le Play first pointed out, there are three elements: the place, the work, and the people; the sociologist's equivalent of environment, function, and organism. Out of the interaction of the folk and their place, through the work, the simple life of the community develops. At the same time, each of these elements carries with it its specific spiritual heritage. The people have their customs and manners and morals and laws; or as we might say more briefly, their institutions; the work has its technology, its craft-experience, from the simple lore of peasant and breeder to the complicated formulæ of the modern chemists and metallurgists; while the deeper perception of the "place," through the analysis of the falling stone, the rising sun, the running water, the decomposing vegetation, and the living animal gives rise to the tradition of "learning" and science.

With this simple outline in mind, the process that created our present mechanical civilization becomes a little more plain; and we can appreciate, perhaps, the difficulties that stand in the way of any swift and easy transformation.

Thus our present order was due to a mingled change in every aspect of the community: morally, it was protestantism; legally, the rise of representative government; socially, the introduction of "democracy"; in custom, the general breakdown of the family unit; industrially, it meant the collapse of the guilds and the growth of the factory-system; scientifically, the spread of physical science, and the increased knowledge of the terrestrial globe—and so on.

Each of these facets of the community's life was the object of separate attention and effort: but it was their totality which produced the modern order. Where—among other reasons—the moral preparation for mechanical civilization was incomplete, as in the Catholic countries, the industrial revolution was also late and incomplete; where the craft-tradition remained strong, as in the beech forests of the Chilterns, the industrial change made fewer inroads into the habits of the community, than, let us say, in Lancashire, where modern industry was untempered and unchallenged.

If the circumstances which hedge in our architecture are to be transformed, it is not sufficient, with Mr. Louis Sullivan, to say that we must ac-

cept and enthrone the virtues of democracy; still
less is there any meaning in the attempt of the Educational Committee of the American Institute of
Architects to educate public taste in the arts. Nor
is there any genuine esthetic salvation in the demand
of the modernists that we embrace in more whole-
hearted fashion the machine. Our architecture has
been full of false starts and unfulfilled promises,
precisely because the ground has not been worked
enough beforehand to receive the new seeds.

If we are to have a fine architecture, we must begin at the other end from that where our sumptu-
ously illustrated magazines on home-building and
architecture begin—not with the building itself, but
with the whole complex out of which architect,
builder, and patron spring, and into which the
finished building, whether it be a cottage or a
skyscraper, is set. Once the conditions are ripe
for a good architecture, the plant will flower by
itself: it did so in the Middle Ages, as a hundred
little towns and villages between Budapest and
Glastonbury still testify; it did so again within a
limited area among the swells of the Renaissance;
and it is springing forth lustily today in the garden
cities of England, the Netherlands, and the Baltic

countries. The notion that our architecture will be improved by courses of appreciation in our museums and colleges is, to put it quite mildly, one of the decadent deceits of snobbery. It is only paper flowers that grow in this fashion

II

In order to get our bearings, we shall pull apart, one by one, the principal elements in our heritage of civilization in the United States, and examine them separately. This is a dangerous convenience, however, and I must emphasize that these strands are tightly intertwined and bound up. It is only in thought that one can take them apart. No one has ever encountered man, save on the earth; no one has ever seen the earth, save through the eyes of a man. There is no logical priority in place, work, and people. In discussing the community one either deals with it as a whole, or one's discussion is incomplete and faulty.

III

The capital sign of the early settlements beyond the seashore was the clearing; and since the great majority of newcomers lived by agriculture, the forest itself appeared merely as an obstacle to be removed. The untouched woods of America were all too lush and generous, and if an occasional Leatherstocking loved them, the new settler saw only land to clear and wood to burn. In the New England village, the tradition of culture was perhaps applied to the land itself, and elsewhere there are occasional elements of good practice, in the ordered neatness of boulder-fences. For the most part, however, the deliberate obliteration of the natural landscape became a great national sport, comparable to the extermination of bison which the casual western traveler devoted himself to at a later date.

The stripping of the Appalachian forest was the first step in our campaign against nature. By 1860 the effect was already grave enough to warn an acute observer, like George Perkins Marsh, of the danger to our civilization, and to prompt him in Earth and Man, to remind his countrymen that other civilizations about the Mediterranean and the Adriatic had lost their top-soil and ruined their agriculture through the wanton destruction of their forests.

In the meanwhile, a new factor had entered. If before the nineteenth century we cleared the forest to make way for the farm, with the entrance of the industrial pioneer we began to clear the farm to parcel out the city. We have called this process the settlement of America, but the name is anomalous, for we formed the habit of using the land, not as a home, a permanent seat of culture, but as a means to something else—principally as a means to the temporary advantages of profitable speculation and exploitation.

James Mackay, a charitable Scotch observer in the middle of the nineteenth century, explained our negligence of the earth by the fact that we pinned our affections to institutions rather than places, and cared not how the landscape was massacred as long as we lived under the same flag and enjoyed the same forms of government. There is no doubt a little truth in this observation; but it was not merely our attachment to republican government that caused this behavior: it was even more, perhaps, our disattachment from the affiliations of a settled life. The pioneer, to put it vulgarly, was on the make and on the move; it did not matter to him how he treated the land, since by the time he could realize its deficiencies he had already escaped to a new virgin area. "What had posterity done for him?"

The pioneers who turned their backs on a civilized way of life in order to extend the boundaries of civilization, left us with a heavy burden—not merely blasted and disorderly landscapes, but the habit of tolerating and producing blasted and disorderly landscapes. As Cobbett pointed out in his attempt to account for the unkempt condition of the American farm, the farmer in this country lacked the example of the great landed estates, where the woods had become cultivated parks, and the meadowland had become lawns. Without this cultivated example in the country, it is no wonder that our cities have been littered, frayed at the edges, ugly; no wonder that our pavements so quickly obliterate trees and grass; no wonder that so many towns are little more than gashes of metal and stone.

Those who had been bred on the land brought into the city none of that disciplined care which might have preserved some of its amenities. They left the smoke of the clearings, which was a sign of rural "progress"; they welcomed the smoke of the towns, and all that accompanied it

It is scarcely a paradox to say that the improvement of our cities must proceed inwards from the countryside; for it is largely a matter of reversing the process which converts the farm into incipient blocks of real estate. Once we assimilate the notion that soil and site have uses quite apart from sale, we shall not continue to barbarize and waste them. Consider how the water's edge of lower Manhattan was developed without the slightest regard for its potential facilities for recreation; how the Acropolis of Pittsburgh, the Hump, was permitted to turn into a noisome slum; how the unique beauty of Casco Bay has been partly secured only by Portland's inferiority as a shipping center. Indeed, all up and down the country one can pick up a thousand examples of towns misplaced, of recreation areas becoming factory sites, of industries located without intelligent reference to raw materials or power or markets or the human beings who serve them, of agricultural land being turned prematurely into suburban lots, and of small rural communities which need the injection of new industries and enterprises, languishing away whilst a metropolis not fifty miles away continues to absorb more people, who daily pay a heavy premium for their congestion.

Architecture and Civilization

I have already drawn attention to the waste of local materials in connection with our manufacture of buildings, our concentration of markets, and our standardization of styles. It is plain that our architects would not have to worry so painfully about the latest fashion-page of architectural tricks, if they had the opportunity to work more consistently with the materials at hand, using brick where clay was plentiful, stone where that was of good quality, and cement where concrete adapted itself to local needs—as it does so well near the seashore, and, for a different reason, in the south. Wood, one of our most important materials for both exterior and interior, has suffered by just the opposite of neglect: so completely have our Appalachian forests been mined, and so expensive are the freight charges for the long haul from the Pacific coast, that good housing in the east depends to no little extent upon our ability to recover continuous local supplies of timber throughout the Appalachian region.

(It is characteristic of our mechanical and metropolitan civilization that one of the great sources of timber waste is the metropolitan newspaper: and one of the remoter blessings of a sounder regional development is that it would, perhaps, remove the hourly itch for the advertising sheet, and by the same token would provide large quantities of wood for housing, without calling for the destruction of ten acres of spruce for the Sunday edition alone! I give the reader the privilege of tracing the pleasant ramifications of this notion.)

To see the interdependence of city and country, to realize that the growth and concentration of one is associated with the depletion and impoverishment of the other, to appreciate that there is a just and harmonious balance between the two—this capacity we have lacked. Before we can build well on any scale we shall, it seems to me, have to develop an art of regional planning, an art which will relate city and countryside in a new pattern from that which was the blind creation of the industrial and the territorial pioneer. Instead of regarding the countryside as so much grist doomed to go eventually into the metropolitan mill, we must plan to preserve and develop all our natural resources to the limit.

It goes without saying that any genuine attempt to provide for the social and economic renewal of a region cannot be constrained to preserve vested land-values and property rights and privileges; indeed, if the land is to be fully loved and cared for again we must recover it in something more than name only. The main objection to keeping our natural resources in the hands of the community, namely, that private capital is more zealous at exploitation, is precisely the reason for urging the first course. Our land has suffered from zeal in exploitation; and it would be much better, for example, that our water power resources should remain temporarily undeveloped, than that they should be incontinently used by private corporations to concentrate population in the centers where a high tariff can be charged. The number of things that are waiting to be done—the planting of town forests, the communal restoration of river banks and beaches, the transformation of bare roads into parkways—will of course differ in each region and locality; and my aim here is only to point to a general objective.

The beginnings of genuine regional planning have already been made in Ontario, Canada, where the social utilization of water-power has directly benefited the rural communities, and given them an independent lease on life. In the United States, Mr.

Benton Mackaye has sketched out a bold and fundamental plan for associating the development of a spinal recreational trail with an electric power development for the whole Appalachian region, along the ridgeway; both trail and power being used as a basis for the re-afforestation and the re-peopling of the whole upland area, with a corresponding decentralization and depopulation of the overcrowded, spotty coastal region. Such a scheme would call for a pretty thorough dislocation of metropolitan values; and if it is slow in making headway, that is only because its gradual institution would mean that a new epoch had begun in American civilization. At the present time it is hard to discover how tangible these new hopes and projects may be: it is significant, however, that the Housing and Regional Planning Commission of the State of New York was called into existence by the necessity for finding a way out of our metropolitan tangle; and it is possible that a new orientation in power and culture is at hand.

In a loose, inconsecutive way, the objectives of regional planning have been dealt with by the conservation movement during the last century; and if the art itself has neither a corpus of experience nor an established body of practitioners, this is only to say that it has, as it were, broken through the surface in a number of places and that it remains to be gathered up and intelligently used. When regional planning starts its active career, it will concern itself to provide a new framework for our communities which will redistribute population and industry, and recultivate the environment—substituting forestry for timber-mining, stable agriculture for soil-mining, and in general the habit of dressing and keeping the earth for our traditional American practice of stripping and deflowering it. Architecture begins historically when the "Bauer" who plants becomes the "Bauer" who builds; and if our architecture is to have a substantial foundation, it is in a refreshened countryside that we will perhaps find it.

IV

Let us now turn to industry. The medieval order was disrupted in America before it could fully take root. As a result we have no craft-tradition that is properly native, with the exception of the shipbuilders and furniture-makers of New England, whose art has been on the wane since the second quarter of the nineteenth century. We have covered up this deficiency by importing from generation to generation foreign workmen, principally Germans and Italians, in whose birthplaces the art of using wood and stone has not been entirely lost; but we are still far from having created an independent craft-tradition of our own. If art is the fine efflorescence of a settled life, invention is the necessity of the roving pioneer who every day faces new difficulties and new hazards; and accordingly we have devoted our energies to the machine, and to the products of the machine. All that we cannot do in this medium we regard as "mere" art, and put it apart from the direct aims and practices of everyday life.

Our skill in working according to exact formulæ with machines and instruments of precision is not to be belittled: socially directed it would put an end to a hundred vapid drudgeries, and it would perhaps give the pervasive finish of a style to structures whose parts are now oddly at sixes and sevens. Unfortunately for us and for the world in general the machine did not come simply as a technological contribution: it appeared when the guild had broken down and when the joint stock company had gotten its piratical start as a Company of Gentleman-Adventurers. As a result, our mechanical age was given an unsocial twist; and inventions which should have worked for the welfare of the community were used for the financial aggrandizement of investors and monopolizers. In architecture, all the skill of the technologist and all the taste of the artist have become subservient to the desire of the financier for a quick turnover of capital, and the ground landlord for the maximum exploitation of the land. The sole chances for good workmanship occur when, by a happy accident of personality or situation, the patron asks of the architect and engineer only the best that they can give.

It is this side of exaggeration to say that today a building is one kind of manufactured product on a counter of manufactured products; but with a difference; for the internal processes of construction are still, in spite of all our advances, handicrafts. An interesting result, as Mr. F. L. Ackermann has pointed out, follows from this fact: namely, that the pace of building tends to lag behind the pace at which other goods are produced under the machine-system; and if this is the case, the quantitative production of buildings is bound to be too low, while their cost is bound, by the same process, to be disproportionately high.

The remedy seized by the engineer, as I have pointed out, is to introduce the process of standardization and mechanization wherever possible. This heightens the pace of building, and by and large it quickens the rate of deterioration in the thing built: both processes increase the turnover of buildings, and so tend to make the art of building approach the rhythm established by our price-system for the other mechanical arts; since, under the price-system, the manufacturer must create a continued demand for his products or risk flooding the market. The two ways of creating a demand are to widen the area of sale or to increase the rate of consumption. Shoddy materials and shoddy workmanship are the most obvious means of accomplishing the second end; but fashion plays a serious part, and maladaptation to use, though less frequently noted, cannot be ignored.

All these little anomalies and inconveniences have come with machinery, not of course because the machine is inherently wasteful and fraudulent, but because our social order has not been adapted to its use. Our gains have been canceled, for the reason that the vast expansion of our productive powers has necessitated an equally vast expansion in our consumptive processes. Hence in many departments of building, the advantage of machinery has been almost nullified; and if handicraft has been driven out, it is less because it is inefficient than because the pace of production and consumption under handicraft is so much retarded.

When Ruskin began to agitate for the revival of handicraft it looked as if our industrial system were bound to triumph everywhere, and as if Ruskin's protest were the last weak chirp of romanticism. At the present time, however, the issue is not so simple as it seemed to the builders of the Crystal Palace; nor are the choices so narrow. What seemed a fugitive philosophy when applied to the machine by itself has turned out to be a rigorous and intelligent criticism, when applied to the machine-system. The use of the machine in provinces where it has no essential concern, the network of relationships that have followed the financial exploitation of machinery— these things have led to a revolt, in which the engineers themselves have participated. It is not machinery alone that causes standardization, we begin to see, but the national market; it is not the machine that makes our cheaper houses blank and anonymous, but the absence of any mediating relation between the user and the designer—except through the personality of the builder, who builds for sale

Apart from this, in certain industries like wood-turning and furniture-making the introduction of the gasoline engine and the electric motor has restored the center of gravity to the small factory, set in the countryside, and to the individual craftsman or group, working in the small shop. Professor Patrick Geddes has characterized the transition from steam to electricity as one from the paleotechnic to the neotechnic order; and intuitive technological geniuses, like Mr. Henry Ford, have been quick to see the possibilities of little factories set in the midst of the countryside. Mechanically speaking, the electric motor has in certain industries and operations placed the individual worker on a par with the multiple-machine factory, even as motor transportation is reducing the advantages of the big city over the small town or village. It is therefore not unreasonable to look forward to a continuation of this development, which will enable groups of building workers to serve their immediate region quite as economically as would a multitude of national factories, producing goods blindly for a blind national market. With direct sale and service, from local sawmills and local furniture-making shops, the older handicrafts themselves might reënter once more through the back door—as indeed they have already begun to do in response to the demands of the wealthy.

I am not suggesting here that handicraft is likely to replace machinery: rather, as Kropotkin said in Fields, Factories and Workshops, machinery itself may lend itself in its modern forms to a more purposive system of production, like that fostered by handicraft; and under this condition the antagonism and disparity between the two forms of production need not be so great as they are at present. In a little valley I happen to be acquainted with, there is enough running water to supply five families with electric light from a single power plant; unfortunately, five families cannot combine for such a purpose in the state I am speaking of without a power-franchise; and so the only source of electric light is a distant commercial power plant using coal. Here is an obvious case where commercial monopoly runs contrary to economy and where the benefits of modern technology are forfeited in the working of our financial system. Once we understand that modern industry does not necessarily bring with it financial and physical concentration, the growth of smaller centers and· a more widespread distribution of the genuine benefits of technology will, I think, take place.

It is true that the movement of the last hundred years has ·been away from handicraft; but a hundred years is a relatively short time, and at least a part of the triumph of machinery has been due to our naïve enjoyment of it as a plaything. There is a wide difference between doing away with hand-labor, as in sawing wood or hoisting a weight, and eliminating handicraft by using machine tools for operations which can be subtly performed only by hand. The first practice is all to the good: the second essentially misunderstands the significance of handicraft and machinery, and I must dwell on this point for a moment, since it is responsible for a good deal of shoddy thinking on the future of art and architecture.

v

On the human side, the prime distinction overlooked by the mechanists is that machine work is principally toil: handicraft, on the other hand, is a form of living. The operations of the mechanical arts are inherently servile, because the worker is forced to keep the pace set by the machine and to follow the pattern set by the designer, someone other than himself; whereas the handicrafts are relatively free, in that they allow a certain leeway to different types of work and different ways of tackling a job. These distinctions are bound up with a difference in the forms that are used; and it is through these esthetic differences that we may, perhaps, best see how the personal and mechanical may be apportioned in the architecture of the future.

The key to handicraft esthetics, it seems to me, is a sort of vital superfluity. The carpenter is not content with his planed surface; nor is the mason satisfied with the smooth stone; nor does the painter impartially cover the bare wall: no, each worker must elaborate the bare utilitarian object until the capital becomes a writhing mass of foliage, until the domed ceiling becomes the gate of heaven, until each object gets the imprint of the fantasies that have ripened in the worker's head. The craftsman literally possesses his work, in the sense that the Bible says a body is possessed by a familiar spirit.

Occasionally, this elaboration passes the point at which it would give the highest esthetic delight to the beholder; nevertheless, the craftsman keeps pouring himself into his job: he must fill up every blank space, and will not be denied, for carving wood or hacking stone, when it is done with a free spirit, is a dignified and enjoyable way of living. Those of us who have become acclimated to industrialism sometimes find the effulgence and profusion of craftsmanship a little bewildering: but if our enjoyment of the portals of a medieval cathedral or the façade of an East Indian house is dulled by the myopic intricacy of the pattern, our appreciation of the craftsman's fun and interest should be heightened. Granting that art is an end in itself, is it not an end to the worker as well as the spectator? A great part of craftsmanship needs no other justification than that it bears the mark of a joyous spirit.

When we compare an ideal product of handicraft, like a Florentine table of the sixteenth century, with an ideal product of mechanical art—say a modern bathroom—the contrasting virtues and defects become plain. The conditions that make possible good machine-work are, first of all, a complete calculation of consequences, embodied in a working drawing or

design: to deviate by a hair's breadth from this calculation is to risk failure. The qualities exemplified
in good machine-work follow naturally from the
implements: they are precision, economy, finish, geo-
metric perfection. When the workman's personality
intervenes in the process, it is carelessness. If he
leave his imprint, it is a flaw.

A good pattern in terms of the machine is one
that fulfills the bare essentials of an object: the
chairishness of a chair, the washiness of a basin, the
enclosedness of a house, and any superfluity that
may be added by way of ornament is a miscarriage
of the machine-process, for by adding dull work to
work that is already dull it defeats the end for which
machinery may legitimately exist in a humane society; namely, to produce a necessary quantity of
useful goods with a minimum of human effort.

Craftsmanship, to put the distinction roughly,
emphasizes the worker's delight in production: anyone who proposed to reduce the amount of time and
effort spent by the carver in wood or stone would be
in effect attempting to shorten the worker's life.
Machine-work, on the other hand, tends at its best
to diminish the inescapable drudgeries of production:
any dodge or decoration that increases the time spent

in service to the machine adds to the physical burden of existence. One is a sufficient end; the other is, legitimately, only a means to an end.

Our modern communities are far from understanding this distinction. Just as in art we multiply inadequate chromolithographs and starve the modern artist, so in architecture a good part of machine-work is devoted to the production of fake handicraft, like the molded stone ornamentation used in huge Renaissance fireplaces, designed frequently for small modern apartments that are superheated by steam. In turn, the surviving worker who now practices handicraft has been debased into a servile drudge, using his skill and love, like his predecessors in Imperial Rome, to copy the original productions of other artists and craftsmen. Between handicraft that is devoted to mechanical reproduction and machinery that is set to reproduce endless simulacra of handicraft, our esthetic opportunities in art and architecture are muffed again and again. An occasional man of talent, like Mr. Samuel Yellin, the iron-worker, will survive; but the great run of craftsmen do not.

Now, with due respect to the slickness and perfection of the best machine-work, we enjoy it because of

the use that it fulfills: it may incidentally achieve
significant form, but no one retains a pickle bottle,
beautifully shaped though Messrs. Heinz and Co.'s
are, for this reason: it was meant for pickles and it
vanishes with the pickles. This is not merely true
of today: it is true of all ages: the common utensils
of life return to the dust, whereas those things that
hold the imprint of man's imagination—the amphoræ
of the Greek potters, the fragile crane-necked bot-
tles of the Persians, the seals of the Egyptians—are
preserved from the rubbish heap, no matter how
frail they may be or how small their intrinsic value.

There is something in man that compels him to
respect the human imprint of art: he lives more
nobly surrounded by his own reflections, as a god
might live. The very rage of iconoclasm which the
Mohammedans and Puritans and eighteenth-century
liberals exhibited betrayed a deep respect for the
power of art; for we destroy the things that threaten
our existence. Art, in a certain sense, is the spiritual
varnish that we lay on material things, to insure
their preservation: on its lowest terms, beauty
is justified because it has "survival value." The
fact that houses which bear the living imprint of
the mind are irreplaceable is what prevents them

from being quickly and callously replaced. Wren's churches are preserved beyond their period of desuetude by Wren's personality. This process is just the opposite to that fostered by the machine-system, and it explains why, in the long run, machine-work may be unsatisfactory and uneconomical—too quickly degraded.

Art, in fact, is one of the main ways in which we escape the vicious circle of economic activity. According to the conventional economist, our economic life has but three phases: production, distribution, and consumption. We work to eat so that we may eat to work. This is a fairly accurate portrait of life in an early industrial town; but it does not apply to the economic processes of a civilized community. Everywhere, even in regions of difficulty, something more comes out of production than the current income and the current saving of capital: sometimes it is leisure and play, sometimes it is religion, philosophy, and science, and sometimes it is art. In the creation of any permanent work of art the processes of dissipation and consumption are stayed: hence the only civilized criterion of a community's economic life is not the amount of things produced, but the durability of things created. A community

with a low rate of production and a high standard
of creation will in the long run be physically richer
than a modern city in which the gains of industry
are frittered away in evanescent, uncreative expenditures. What matters is the ratio of production
to creation.

Here lies the justification of the modern architect.
Cut off though he is from the actual processes of
building, he nevertheless remains the sole surviving
craftsman who maintains the relation towards the
whole structure that the old handicraft workers used
to enjoy in connection with their particular job.
The architect can still leave his imprint, and even
in the severely utilitarian factory he can take the
simple forms of the engineer and turn them into a
superb structure like Messrs. Helmle and Corbett's
Fletcher Building in New York. To the extent that
honest engineering is better than fake architecture,
genuine architecture is better than engineering: for
it strikes the same esthetic and humane chord that
painting and sculpture appeal to by themselves. The
freedom to depart from arbitrary and mechanical
precedent, the freedom to project new forms which
will more adequately meet his problem are essential
to the architect. Up to the present he has been

able, for the most part, to exercise this freedom only on traditional buildings, like churches and libraries and auditoriums, which are outside the reaches of the present commercial regime and have therefore some prospect of durability.

But before the whole mass of contemporary building will be ready to receive the imprint of the architect, and before the handicrafts re-enter the modern building to give the luster of permanence to its decorations and fixtures, there will have to be a pretty thoroughgoing reorientation in our economic life. Whilst buildings are erected to increase site values, whilst houses are produced in block to be sold to the first wretch who must put a roof over his family's head, it is useless to dwell upon the ministrations of art; and, unfortunately, too much of our building today rests upon this basis and exhibits all the infirmities of our present economic structure.

From the aspect of our well-to-do suburbs and our newly-planned industrial towns, from the beginnings of a sound functional architecture in some of our schools and factories, it is easy to see what the architecture of our various regions might be if it had the opportunity to work itself out in a coherent

pattern. For the present, however, it is impossible
to say with any certainty whether our architects are
doomed to be extruded by mechanism, or whether
they will have the opportunity to restore to our
machine-system some of the freedom of an earlier
regime; and I have no desire to burden this discussion with predictions and exhortations. But if the
conclusions we have reached are sound, it is only the
second possibility that holds out any promise to the
good life.

VI

So far we have considered the regional and
industrial bearing of architecture: it now remains
to examine briefly its relation to the community
itself.

In the building of our cities and villages the main
mores we have carried over have been those of the
pioneer. We have seen how the animus of the pioneer, "mine and move," is antagonistic to the settled
life out of which ordered industries and a great
architecture grow. We have seen also how this
animus was deepened in the nineteenth century by
the extraordinary temptation to profit by the increase in land-increments which followed the growth

of population, the result being, as Mr. Henry George saw when he came back to the cities of the East from a part of California that was still in the throes of settlement—progress *and* poverty.

Now, to increase the population of a town and to raise the nominal values in ground rents is almost a moral imperative in our American communities. That is why our zoning laws, which attempt to regulate the use of land and provide against unfair competition in obtaining the unearned increment, almost universally leave a loophole through which the property owners, by mutual consent, may transform the character of the neighborhood for more intensive uses and higher ground rents. All our city planning, and more and more our architecture itself, is done with reference to prospective changes in the value of real estate. It is nothing to the real estate speculator that the growth of a city destroys the very purpose for which it may legitimately exist, as the growth of Atlantic City into a suburb of Broadway and Chestnut Street ruined its charm as a seaside fishing village. Sufficient unto the day is the evil he creates.

Most of the important changes that must be effected in relation to industry and the land cannot

be accomplished without departing from these dominant *mores*—from the customs and laws and uneasy
standards of ethics which we carry over from the
days of our continental conquest. The pioneer inheritance of the miner, coupled with the imperial
inheritance of the hunter-warrior, out for loot, lie
at the bottom of our present-day social structure;
and it is useless to expect any vital changes in the
milieu of architecture until the miner and the hunter
are subordinated to relatively more civilized types,
concerned with the culture of life, rather than with
its exploitation and destruction.

I am aware that the statement of the problem
in these elementary terms will seem a little crude and
unfamiliar in America where, in the midst of our
buzzing urban environment, we lose sight of the
underlying primitive reality, or—which is worse—
speak vaguely of the "cave-man" unleashed in modern civilization. I do not deny that there are other
elements in our makeup and situation that play an
important part; but it is enough to bring forward
here the notion that our concern with physical
utilities and with commercial values is something
more than an abstract defect in our philosophy. On
the contrary, it seems to me to inhere in the domi-

nant occupations of the country, and it is less to
be overcome by moralizing and exhortation, than to
be grown out of, by taking pains to provide for the
ascendancy and renewal of the more humane occupations.

Our communities have grown blindly, and, escaping
the natural limitations which curbed even the Roman
engineers, have not been controlled, on the other
hand, by any normative ideal. One step in the direction of departing from our pioneer customs and
habits would be to consider what the nature of a
city is, and what functions it performs. The dominant, abstract culture of the nineteenth century
was blithely unconcerned with these questions, but,
as I have already pointed out, the Puritans not
merely recognized their importance, but regulated
the plan and layout of the city accordingly. The
notion that there is anything arbitrary in imposing
a limitation upon the area and population of a city
is absurd: the limits have already been laid down
in the physical conditions of human nature, as Mr.
Frederic Harrison once wisely observed, in the fact
that men do not walk comfortably faster than three
miles an hour, nor can they spend on the physical
exertion of locomotion and exercise more than a

few hours in every twenty-four. With respect to the needs of recreation, home-life, and health, the growth of a city to the point where the outlying citizen must travel two hours a day in the subway between his office and his place of work is unintelligent and arbitrary.

A city, properly speaking, does not exist by the accretion of houses, but by the association of human beings. When the accretion of houses reaches such a point of congestion or expansion that human association becomes difficult, the place ceases to be a city. The institutions that make up the city— schools, clubs, libraries, gymnasia, theaters, churches, and so forth—can be traced in one form or another back to the primitive community: they function on the basis of immediate intercourse, and they can serve through their individual units only a limited number of people. Should the population of a local community be doubled, all its civic equipment must be doubled too; otherwise the life that functions through these institutions and opportunities will lapse and disappear.

It is not my purpose to discuss in detail the various devices by which our practice of endless growth and unlimited increment may be limited. Once the necessary conversion in faith and morals has taken place, the other things will come easily: for example, the social appropriation of unearned land-increments, and the exercise of the town-planner's art to limit the tendency of a community to straggle beyond its boundaries.

While a great many other ideas and measures are of prime importance for the good life of the community, that which concerns its architectural expression is the notion of the community as limited in numbers, and in area; and as formed, not merely by the agglomeration of people, but by their relation to definite social and economic institutions. To express these relations clearly, to embody them in buildings and roads and gardens in which each individual structure will be subordinated to the whole —this is the end of community planning.

With the coherence and stability indicated by this method of planning, architectural effect would not lie in the virtuosity of the architect or in the peculiar ornateness and originality of any particular building: it would tend to be diffused, so that the humblest shop would share in the triumph with the most conspicuous public building. There are examples of this order of comprehensive architectural design

in hundreds of little villages and towns in pre-industrial Europe—to say nothing of a good handful in
pre-industrial America—and community planning
would make it once more our daily practice. That
it can be done again the examples of Letchworth
and Welwyn in England, and numerous smaller gar-
dened cities created by municipal authorities in
England and other parts of Europe, bear evidence;
and where the precepts of Mr. Ebenezer Howard
have been to any degree followed, architecture has
been quick to benefit.

The difference between community planning and
the ordinary method of city-extension and suburb-
building has been very well put in a recent report
to the American Institute of Architects, by the Committee on Community Planning. "Community planning," says the report, "does not ask by what des-
perate means a city of 600,000 people can add
another 400,000 during the next generation, nor how
a city of seven millions may enlarge its effective borders to include 29,000,000. It begins, rather, at the
other end, and it asks with Mr. Ebenezer Howard
how big must a city be to perform all of its social,
educational, and industrial functions. It attempts
to establish minima and maxima for different kinds

of communities, depending upon their character and function. If the established practices of industry, commerce, and finance tend to produce monstrous agglomerations which do not contribute to human welfare or happiness, community planning must question these established practices, since the values they create have nothing to do with the essential welfare of the community itself, and since the condition thus created is inimical to the stable, architectural development of the community."

The normative idea of the garden-city and the garden-village is the corrective for the flatulent and inorganic conception of city-development that we labor with, and under, today. So far from being a strange importation from Europe, the garden-city is nothing more or less than a sophisticated recovery of a form that we once enjoyed on our Atlantic seaboard, and lost through our sudden and almost uncontrollable access of natural resources and people. Here and there an enterprising and somewhat benevolent industrial corporation has attempted to carry out some of the principles of garden-city development; and the United States Housing Corporation and the Shipping Board had begun to build many admirable communities, when the war brought this vast initiative to an end. These precedents are better than nothing, it goes without saying, but there will have to be a pretty thorough reorientation in our economic and social life before the garden-city will be anything more than a slick phrase, without content or power.

Until our communities are ready to undertake the sort of community planning that leads to garden-cities, it will be empty eloquence to talk about the future of American architecture. Sheltered as an enjoyment for the prosperous minority, or used as a skysign for the advertisement of business, architecture will still await its full opportunity for creative achievement.

The signs of promise are plenty, and if I have dealt with the darker side of the picture and have occasionally overemphasized the weaknesses and defects of the American tradition, it is only because in our present appreciation of what the American architect has already given form to, we are likely to forget the small area these achievements occupy. So far we have achieved patches of good building; more than once we have achieved the *mot juste*, but we have not learnt the more difficult art of consecutive discourse. With respect to the architecture of the whole community, medieval Boston and medieval New Amsterdam had more to boast than their magnificently endowed successors. Just as Mr. Babbitt's great ancestor, Scadder, transformed a swamp into a thriving metropolis by the simple method of calling it New Eden, so do we tend to lighten our burdens by calling them the "blessings of progress"; but it does not avail. Our mechanical and metropolitan civilization, with all its genuine advances, has let certain essential human elements drop out of its scheme; and until we recover these elements our civilization will be at loose ends, and our architecture will unerringly express this situation.

Home, meeting-place, and factory; polity, culture, and art have still to be united and wrought together, and this task is one of the fundamental tasks of our civilization. Once that union is effected, the long breach between art and life, which began with the Renaissance, will be brought to an end. The magnitude of our task might seem a little disheartening, were it not for the fact that, "against or with our will," our civilization is perpetually being modified and altered. If in less than a hundred years the feudal civilization of Japan could adopt our modern mechanical gear, there is nothing to prevent our own civilization from recovering once more its human base—nothing, that is, except our own desires, aims, habits, and ends. This is an ironic consolation, perhaps, but the remedy it offers is real.

ENVOI

The aristocracies of the world have never doubted the supremacy of the home and garden and temple over all the baser mechanisms of existence, and the folk-civilizations out of which aristocracies have so often risen have never strayed far from these realities. In the Norse fables, the dwarfs are regarded as queer monsters, because they are always "busy people" who have no pride or joy except in the work they perform and the mischief they cause.

The great heresy of the modern world is that it ceased to worship the Lords of Life, who made the rivers flow, caused the animals to mate, and brought forth the yearly miracle of vegetation: it prostrated itself, on the contrary, before the dwarfs, with their mechanical ingenuity, and the giants, with their imbecile power. Today our lives are perpetually menaced by these "busy people"; we are surrounded by their machines, and for worship, we turn their prayer wheels of red-tape.

It will not always be so; that would be monstrous.

Sticks and Stones

Sooner or later we will learn to pick our way out of the débris that the dwarfs, the gnomes, and the giants have created; eventually, to use Henry Adams' figure, the sacred mother will supplant the dynamo. The prospects for our architecture are bound up with a new orientation towards the things that are symbolized in the home, the garden and the temple; for architecture sums up the civilization it enshrines, and the mass of our buildings can never be better or worse than the institutions that have shaped them.

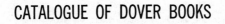

CATALOGUE OF DOVER BOOKS

Books Explaining Science and Mathematics

WHAT IS SCIENCE?, N. Campbell. The role of experiment and measurement, the function of mathematics, the nature of scientific laws, the difference between laws and theories, the limitations of science, and many similarly provocative topics are treated clearly and without technicalities by an eminent scientist. "Still an excellent introduction to scientific philosophy," H. Margenau in PHYSICS TODAY. "A first-rate primer . . . deserves a wide audience," SCIENTIFIC AMERICAN. 192pp. 5⅜ x 8.   S43 Paperbound **$1.25**

THE NATURE OF PHYSICAL THEORY, P. W. Bridgman. A Nobel Laureate's clear, non-technical lectures on difficulties and paradoxes connected with frontier research on the physical sciences. Concerned with such central concepts as thought, logic, mathematics, relativity, probability, wave mechanics, etc. he analyzes the contributions of such men as Newton, Einstein, Bohr, Heisenberg, and many others. "Lucid and entertaining . . . recommended to anyone who wants to get some insight into current philosophies of science," THE NEW PHILOSOPHY. Index. xi + 138pp. 5⅜ x 8.   S33 Paperbound **$1.25**

EXPERIMENT AND THEORY IN PHYSICS, Max Born. A Nobel Laureate examines the nature of experiment and theory in theoretical physics and analyzes the advances made by the great physicists of our day: Heisenberg, Einstein, Bohr, Planck, Dirac, and others. The actual process of creation is detailed step-by-step by one who participated. A fine examination of the scientific method at work. 44pp. 5⅜ x 8.   S308 Paperbound **75¢**

THE PSYCHOLOGY OF INVENTION IN THE MATHEMATICAL FIELD, J. Hadamard. The reports of such men as Descartes, Pascal, Einstein, Poincaré, and others are considered in this investigation of the method of idea-creation in mathematics and other sciences and the thinking process in general. How do ideas originate? What is the role of the unconscious? What is Poincaré's forgetting hypothesis? are some of the fascinating questions treated. A penetrating analysis of Einstein's thought processes concludes the book. xiii + 145pp. 5⅜ x 8.   T107 Paperbound **$1.25**

THE NATURE OF LIGHT AND COLOUR IN THE OPEN AIR, M. Minnaert. Why are shadows sometimes blue, sometimes green, or other colors depending on the light and surroundings? What causes mirages? Why do multiple suns and moons appear in the sky? Professor Minnaert explains these unusual phenomena and hundreds of others in simple, easy-to-understand terms based on optical laws and the properties of light and color. No mathematics is required but artists, scientists, students, and everyone fascinated by these "tricks" of nature will find thousands of useful and amazing pieces of information. Hundreds of observational experiments are suggested which require no special equipment. 200 illustrations; 42 photos. xvi + 362pp. 5⅜ x 8.   T196 Paperbound **$2.00**

THE UNIVERSE OF LIGHT, W. Bragg. Sir William Bragg, Nobel Laureate and great modern physicist, is also well known for his powers of clear exposition. Here he analyzes all aspects of light for the layman: lenses, reflection, refraction, the optics of vision, x-rays, the photoelectric effect, etc. He tells you what causes the color of spectra, rainbows, and soap bubbles, how magic mirrors work, and much more. Dozens of simple experiments are described. Preface. Index. 199 line drawings and photographs, including 2 full-page color plates. x + 283pp. 5⅜ x 8.   T538 Paperbound **$1.85**

SOAP-BUBBLES: THEIR COLOURS AND THE FORCES THAT MOULD THEM, C. V. Boys. For continuing popularity and validity as scientific primer, few books can match this volume of easily-followed experiments, explanations. Lucid exposition of complexities of liquid films, surface tension and related phenomena, bubbles' reaction to heat, motion, music, magnetic fields. Experiments with capillary attraction, soap bubbles on frames, composite bubbles, liquid cylinders and jets, bubbles other than soap, etc. Wonderful introduction to scientific method, natural laws that have many ramifications in areas of modern physics. Only complete edition in print. New Introduction by S. Z. Lewin, New York University. 83 illustrations; 1 full-page color plate. xii + 190pp. 5⅜ x 8½.   T542 Paperbound **95¢**

THE STORY OF X-RAYS FROM RONTGEN TO ISOTOPES, A. R. Bleich, M.D. This book, by a member of the American College of Radiology, gives the scientific explanation of x-rays, their applications in medicine, industry and art, and their danger (and that of atmospheric radiation) to the individual and the species. You learn how radiation therapy is applied against cancer, how x-rays diagnose heart disease and other ailments, how they are used to examine mummies for information on diseases of early societies, and industrial materials for hidden weaknesses. 54 illustrations show x-rays of flowers, bones, stomach, gears with flaws, etc. 1st publication. Index. xix + 186pp. 5⅜ x 8.   T622 Paperbound **$1.35**

SPINNING TOPS AND GYROSCOPIC MOTION, John Perry. A classic elementary text of the dynamics of rotation — the behavior and use of rotating bodies such as gyroscopes and tops. In simple, everyday English you are shown how quasi-rigidity is induced in discs of paper, smoke rings, chains, etc., by rapid motions; why a gyrostat falls and why a top rises; precession; how the earth's motion affects climate; and many other phenomena. Appendix on practical use of gyroscopes. 62 figures. 128pp. 5⅜ x 8.   T416 Paperbound **$1.00**

SNOW CRYSTALS, W. A. Bentley, M. J. Humphreys. For almost 50 years W. A. Bentley photographed snow flakes in his laboratory in Jericho, Vermont; in 1931 the American Meteorological Society gathered together the best of his work, some 2400 photographs of snow flakes, plus a few ice flowers, windowpane frosts, dew, frozen rain, and other ice formations. Pictures were selected for beauty and scientific value. A very valuable work to anyone in meteorology, cryology; most interesting to layman; extremely useful for artist who wants beautiful, crystalline designs. All copyright free. Unabridged reprint of 1931 edition. 2453 illustrations. 227pp. 8 x 10½.   T287 Paperbound **$3.00**

A DOVER SCIENCE SAMPLER, edited by George Barkin. A collection of brief, non-technical passages from 44 Dover Books Explaining Science for the enjoyment of the science-minded browser. Includes work of Bertrand Russell, Poincaré, Laplace, Max Born, Galileo, Newton; material on physics, mathematics, metallurgy, anatomy, astronomy, chemistry, etc. You will be fascinated by Martin Gardner's analysis of the sincere pseudo-scientist, Moritz's account of Newton's absentmindedness, Bernard's examples of human vivisection, etc. Illustrations from the Diderot Pictorial Encyclopedia and De Re Metallica. 64 pages.   **FREE**

THE STORY OF ATOMIC THEORY AND ATOMIC ENERGY, J. G. Feinberg. A broader approach to subject of nuclear energy and its cultural implications than any other similar source. Very readable, informal, completely non-technical text. Begins with first atomic theory, 600 B.C. and carries you through the work of Mendelejeff, Röntgen, Madame Curie, to Einstein's equation and the A-bomb. New chapter goes through thermonuclear fission, binding energy, other events up to 1959. Radioactive decay and radiation hazards, future benefits, work of Bohr, moderns, hundreds more topics. "Deserves special mention . . . not only authoritative but thoroughly popular in the best sense of the word," Saturday Review. Formerly, "The Atom Story." Expanded with new chapter. Three appendixes. Index. 34 illustrations. vii + 243pp. 5⅜ x 8.   T625 Paperbound **$1.60**

THE STRANGE STORY OF THE QUANTUM, AN ACCOUNT FOR THE GENERAL READER OF THE GROWTH OF IDEAS UNDERLYING OUR PRESENT ATOMIC KNOWLEDGE, B. Hoffmann. Presents lucidly and expertly, with barest amount of mathematics, the problems and theories which led to modern quantum physics. Dr. Hoffmann begins with the closing years of the 19th century, when certain trifling discrepancies were noticed, and with illuminating analogies and examples takes you through the brilliant concepts of Planck, Einstein, Pauli, Broglie, Bohr, Schroedinger, Heisenberg, Dirac, Sommerfeld, Feynman, etc. This edition includes a new, long postscript carrying the story through 1958. "Of the books attempting an account of the history and contents of our modern atomic physics which have come to my attention, this is the best," H. Margenau, Yale University, in "American Journal of Physics." 32 tables and line illustrations. Index. 275pp. 5⅜ x 8.   T518 Paperbound **$1.50**

SPACE AND TIME, E. Borel. Written by a versatile mathematician of world renown with his customary lucidity and precision, this introduction to relativity for the layman presents scores of examples, analogies, and illustrations that open up new ways of thinking about space and time. It covers abstract geometry and geographical maps, continuity and topology, the propagation of light, the special theory of relativity, the general theory of relativity, theoretical researches, and much more. Mathematical notes. 2 Indexes. 4 Appendices. 15 figures. xvi + 243pp. 5⅜ x 8.   T592 Paperbound **$1.45**

FROM EUCLID TO EDDINGTON: A STUDY OF THE CONCEPTIONS OF THE EXTERNAL WORLD, Sir Edmund Whittaker. A foremost British scientist traces the development of theories of natural philosophy from the western rediscovery of Euclid to Eddington, Einstein, Dirac, etc. The inadequacy of classical physics is contrasted with present day attempts to understand the physical world through relativity, non-Euclidean geometry, space curvature, wave mechanics, etc. 5 major divisions of examination: Space; Time and Movement; the Concepts of Classical Physics; the Concepts of Quantum Mechanics; the Eddington Universe. 212pp. 5⅜ x 8.   T491 Paperbound **$1.35**

Nature, Biology

NATURE RECREATION: Group Guidance for the Out-of-doors, William Gould Vinal. Intended for both the uninitiated nature instructor and the education student on the college level, this complete "how-to" program surveys the entire area of nature education for the young. Philosophy of nature recreation; requirements, responsibilities, important information for group leaders; nature games; suggested group projects; conducting meetings and getting discussions started; etc. Scores of immediately applicable teaching aids, plus completely updated sources of information, pamphlets, field guides, recordings, etc. Bibliography. 74 photographs. + 310pp. 5⅜ x 8½. **T1015 Paperbound $1.75**

HOW TO KNOW THE WILD FLOWERS, Mrs. William Starr Dana. Classic nature book that has introduced thousands to wonders of American wild flowers. Color-season principle of organization is easy to use, even by those with no botanical training, and the genial, refreshing discussions of history, folklore, uses of over 1,000 native and escape flowers, foliage plants are informative as well as fun to read. Over 170 full-page plates, collected from several editions, may be colored in to make permanent records of finds. Revised to conform with 1950 edition of Gray's Manual of Botany. xlii + 438pp. 5⅜ x 8½. **T332 Paperbound $2.00**

HOW TO KNOW THE FERNS, F. T. Parsons. Ferns, among our most lovely native plants, are all too little known. This classic of nature lore will enable the layman to identify almost any American fern he may come across. After an introduction on the structure and life of ferns, the 57 most important ferns are fully pictured and described (arranged upon a simple identification key). Index of Latin and English names. 61 illustrations and 42 full-page plates. xiv + 215pp. 5⅜ x 8. **T740 Paperbound $1.35**

MANUAL OF THE TREES OF NORTH AMERICA, Charles Sprague Sargent. Still unsurpassed as most comprehensive, reliable study of North American tree characteristics, precise locations and distribution. By dean of American dendrologists. Every tree native to U.S., Canada, Alaska, 185 genera, 717 species, described in detail—leaves, flowers, fruit, winterbuds, bark, wood, growth habits etc. plus discussion of varieties and local variants, immaturity variations. Over 100 keys, including unusual 11-page analytical key to genera, aid in identification. 783 clear illustrations of flowers, fruit, leaves. An unmatched permanent reference work for all nature lovers. Second enlarged (1926) edition. Synopsis of families. Analytical key to genera. Glossary of technical terms. Index. 783 illustrations, 1 map. Two volumes. Total of 982pp. 5⅜ x 8. **T277 Vol. I Paperbound $2.25**
T278 Vol. II Paperbound $2.25
The set $4.50

TREES OF THE EASTERN AND CENTRAL UNITED STATES AND CANADA, W. M. Harlow. A revised edition of a standard middle-level guide to native trees and important escapes. More than 140 trees are described in detail, and illustrated with more than 600 drawings and photographs. Supplementary keys will enable the careful reader to identify almost any tree he might encounter. xiii + 288pp. 5⅜ x 8. **T395 Paperbound $1.35**

GUIDE TO SOUTHERN TREES, Ellwood S. Harrar and J. George Harrar. All the essential information about trees indigenous to the South, in an extremely handy format. Introductory essay on methods of tree classification and study, nomenclature, chief divisions of Southern trees, etc. Approximately 100 keys and synopses allow for swift, accurate identification of trees. Numerous excellent illustrations, non-technical text make this a useful book for teachers of biology or natural science, nature lovers, amateur naturalists. Revised 1962 edition. Index. Bibliography. Glossary of technical terms. 920 illustrations; 201 full-page plates. ix + 709pp. 4⅝ x 6⅜. **T945 Paperbound $2.35**

FRUIT KEY AND TWIG KEY TO TREES AND SHRUBS, W. M. Harlow. Bound together in one volume for the first time, these handy and accurate keys to fruit and twig identification are the only guides of their sort with photographs (up to 3 times natural size). "Fruit Key": Key to over 120 different deciduous and evergreen fruits. 139 photographs and 11 line drawings. Synoptic summary of fruit types. Bibliography. 2 Indexes (common and scientific names). "Twig Key": Key to over 160 different twigs and buds. 173 photographs. Glossary of technical terms. Bibliography. 2 Indexes (common and scientific names). Two volumes bound as one. Total of xvii + 126pp. 5⅝ x 8⅜. **T511 Paperbound $1.25**

INSECT LIFE AND INSECT NATURAL HISTORY, S. W. Frost. A work emphasizing habits, social life, and ecological relations of insects, rather than more academic aspects of classification and morphology. Prof. Frost's enthusiasm and knowledge are everywhere evident as he discusses insect associations and specialized habits like leaf-rolling, leaf-mining, and case-making, the gall insects, the boring insects, aquatic insects, etc. He examines all sorts of matters not usually covered in general works, such as: insects as human food, insect music and musicians, insect response to electric and radio waves, use of insects in art and literature. The admirably executed purpose of this book, which covers the middle ground between elementary treatment and scholarly monographs, is to excite the reader to observe for himself. Over 700 illustrations. Extensive bibliography. x + 524pp. 5⅜ x 8. **T517 Paperbound $2.45**

COMMON SPIDERS OF THE UNITED STATES, J. H. Emerton. Here is a nature hobby you can pursue right in your own cellar! Only non-technical, but thorough, reliable guide to spiders for the layman. Over 200 spiders from all parts of the country, arranged by scientific classification, are identified by shape and color, number of eyes, habitat and range, habits, etc. Full text, 501 line drawings and photographs, and valuable introduction explain webs, poisons, threads, capturing and preserving spiders, etc. Index. New synoptic key by S. W. Frost. xxiv + 225pp. 5⅜ x 8.   T223 Paperbound $1.45

THE LIFE STORY OF THE FISH: HIS MANNERS AND MORALS, Brian Curtis. A comprehensive, non-technical survey of just about everything worth knowing about fish. Written for the aquarist, the angler, and the layman with an inquisitive mind, the text covers such topics as evolution, external covering and protective coloration, physics and physiology of vision, maintenance of equilibrium, function of the lateral line canal for auditory and temperature senses, nervous system, function of the air bladder, reproductive system and methods—courtship, mating, spawning, care of young—and many more. Also sections on game fish, the problems of conservation and a fascinating chapter on fish curiosities. "Clear, simple language . . . excellent judgment in choice of subjects . . . delightful sense of humor," New York Times. Revised (1949) edition. Index. Bibliography of 72 items. 6 full-page photographic plates. xii + 284pp. 5⅜ x 8.   T929 Paperbound $1.65

BATS, Glover Morrill Allen. The most comprehensive study of bats as a life-form by the world's foremost authority. A thorough summary of just about everything known about this fascinating and mysterious flying mammal, including its unique location sense, hibernation and cycles, its habitats and distribution, its wing structure and flying habits, and its relationship to man in the long history of folklore and superstition. Written on a middle-level, the book can be profitably studied by a trained zoologist and thoroughly enjoyed by the layman. "An absorbing text with excellent illustrations. Bats should have more friends and fewer thoughtless detractors as a result of the publication of this volume," William Beebe, Books. Extensive bibliography. 57 photographs and illustrations. x + 368pp. 5⅜ x 8½.
T984 Paperbound $2.00

BIRDS AND THEIR ATTRIBUTES, Glover Morrill Allen. A fine general introduction to birds as living organisms, especially valuable because of emphasis on structure, physiology, habits, behavior. Discusses relationship of bird to man, early attempts at scientific ornithology, feathers and coloration, skeletal structure including bills, legs and feet, wings. Also food habits, evolution and present distribution, feeding and nest-building, still unsolved questions of migrations and location sense, many more similar topics. Final chapter on classification, nomenclature. A good popular-level summary for the biologist; a first-rate introduction for the layman. Reprint of 1925 edition. References and index. 51 illustrations. viii + 338pp. 5⅜ x 8½.   T957 Paperbound $1.85

LIFE HISTORIES OF NORTH AMERICAN BIRDS, Arthur Cleveland Bent. Bent's monumental series of books on North American birds, prepared and published under auspices of Smithsonian Institute, is the definitive coverage of the subject, the most-used single source of information. Now the entire set is to be made available by Dover in inexpensive editions. This encyclopedic collection of detailed, specific observations utilizes reports of hundreds of contemporary observers, writings of such naturalists as Audubon, Burroughs, William Brewster, as well as author's own extensive investigations. Contains literally everything known about life history of each bird considered: nesting, eggs, plumage, distribution and migration, voice, enemies, courtship, etc. These not over-technical works are musts for ornithologists, conservationists, amateur naturalists, anyone seriously interested in American birds.

BIRDS OF PREY. More than 100 subspecies of hawks, falcons, eagles, buzzards, condors and owls, from the common barn owl to the extinct caracara of Guadaloupe Island. 400 photographs. Two volume set. Index for each volume. Bibliographies of 403, 520 items. 197 full-page plates. Total of 907pp. 5⅜ x 8½.   Vol. I T931 Paperbound $2.50
                                                            Vol. II T932 Paperbound $2.50

WILD FOWL. Ducks, geese, swans, and tree ducks—73 different subspecies. Two volume set. Index for each volume. Bibliographies of 124, 144 items. 106 full-page plates. Total of 685pp. 5⅜ x 8½.   Vol. I T285 Paperbound $2.50
                                                            Vol. II T286 Paperbound $2.50

SHORE BIRDS. 81 varieties (sandpipers, woodcocks, plovers, snipes, phalaropes, curlews, oyster catchers, etc.). More than 200 photographs of eggs, nesting sites, adult and young of important species. Two volume set. Index for each volume. Bibliographies of 261, 188 items. 121 full-page plates. Total of 860pp. 5⅜ x 8½.   Vol. I T933 Paperbound $2.35
                                                            Vol. II T934 Paperbound $2.35

THE LIFE OF PASTEUR, R. Vallery-Radot. 13th edition of this definitive biography, cited in Encyclopaedia Britannica. Authoritative, scholarly, well-documented with contemporary quotes, observations; gives complete picture of Pasteur's personal life; especially thorough presentation of scientific activities with silkworms, fermentation, hydrophobia, inoculation, etc. Introduction by Sir William Osler. Index. 505pp. 5⅜ x 8.   T632 Paperbound $2.00

Puzzles, Mathematical Recreations

SYMBOLIC LOGIC and THE GAME OF LOGIC, Lewis Carroll. "Symbolic Logic" is not concerned with modern symbolic logic, but is instead a collection of over 380 problems posed with charm and imagination, using the syllogism, and a fascinating diagrammatic method of drawing conclusions. In "The Game of Logic" Carroll's whimsical imagination devises a logical game played with 2 diagrams and counters (included) to manipulate hundreds of tricky syllogisms. The final section, "Hit or Miss" is a lagniappe of 101 additional puzzles in the delightful Carroll manner. Until this reprint edition, both of these books were rarities costing up to $15 each. Symbolic Logic: Index. xxxi + 199pp. The Game of Logic: 96pp. 2 vols. bound as one. 5⅜ x 8. T492 Paperbound **$1.50**

PILLOW PROBLEMS and A TANGLED TALE, Lewis Carroll. One of the rarest of all Carroll's works, "Pillow Problems" contains 72 original math puzzles, all typically ingenious. Particularly fascinating are Carroll's answers which remain exactly as he thought them out, reflecting his actual mental process. The problems in "A Tangled Tale" are in story form, originally appearing as a monthly magazine serial. Carroll not only gives the solutions, but uses answers sent in by readers to discuss wrong approaches and misleading paths, and grades them for insight. Both of these books were rarities until this edition, "Pillow Problems" costing up to $25, and "A Tangled Tale" $15. Pillow Problems: Preface and Introduction by Lewis Carroll. xx + 109pp. A Tangled Tale: 6 illustrations. 152pp. Two vols. bound as one. 5⅜ x 8. T493 Paperbound **$1.50**

AMUSEMENTS IN MATHEMATICS, Henry Ernest Dudeney. The foremost British originator of mathematical puzzles is always intriguing, witty, and paradoxical in this classic, one of the largest collections of mathematical amusements. More than 430 puzzles, problems, and paradoxes. Mazes and games, problems on number manipulation, unicursal and other route problems, puzzles on measuring, weighing, packing, age, kinship, chessboards, joiners', crossing river, plane figure dissection, and many others. Solutions. More than 450 illustrations. vii + 258pp. 5⅜ x 8. T473 Paperbound **$1.25**

THE CANTERBURY PUZZLES, Henry Dudeney. Chaucer's pilgrims set one another problems in story form. Also Adventures of the Puzzle Club, the Strange Escape of the King's Jester, the Monks of Riddlewell, the Squire's Christmas Puzzle Party, and others. All puzzles are original, based on dissecting plane figures, arithmetic, algebra, elementary calculus and other branches of mathematics, and purely logical ingenuity. "The limit of ingenuity and intricacy," The Observer. Over 110 puzzles. Full Solutions. 150 illustrations. vii + 225pp. 5⅜ x 8. T474 Paperbound **$1.25**

MATHEMATICAL EXCURSIONS, H. A. Merrill. Even if you hardly remember your high school math, you'll enjoy the 90 stimulating problems contained in this book and you will come to understand a great many mathematical principles with surprisingly little effort. Many useful shortcuts and diversions not generally known are included: division by inspection, Russian peasant multiplication, memory systems for pi, building odd and even magic squares, square roots by geometry, dyadic systems, and many more. Solutions to difficult problems. 50 illustrations. 145pp. 5⅜ x 8. T350 Paperbound **$1.00**

MAGIC SQUARES AND CUBES, W. S. Andrews. Only book-length treatment in English, a thorough non-technical description and analysis. Here are nasik, overlapping, pandiagonal, serrated squares; magic circles, cubes, spheres, rhombuses. Try your hand at 4-dimensional magical figures! Much unusual folklore and tradition included. High school algebra is sufficient. 754 diagrams and illustrations. viii + 419pp. 5⅜ x 8. T658 Paperbound **$1.85**

CALIBAN'S PROBLEM BOOK: MATHEMATICAL, INFERENTIAL AND CRYPTOGRAPHIC PUZZLES, H. Phillips (Caliban), S. T. Shovelton, G. S. Marshall. 105 ingenious problems by the greatest living creator of puzzles based on logic and inference. Rigorous, modern, piquant; reflecting their author's unusual personality, these intermediate and advanced puzzles all involve the ability to reason clearly through complex situations; some call for mathematical knowledge, ranging from algebra to number theory. Solutions. xi + 180pp. 5⅜ x 8. T736 Paperbound **$1.25**

MATHEMATICAL PUZZLES FOR BEGINNERS AND ENTHUSIASTS, G. Mott-Smith. 188 mathematical puzzles based on algebra, dissection of plane figures, permutations, and probability, that will test and improve your powers of inference and interpretation. The Odic Force, The Spider's Cousin, Ellipse Drawing, theory and strategy of card and board games like tit-tat-toe, go moku, salvo, and many others. 100 pages of detailed mathematical explanations. Appendix of primes, square roots, etc. 135 illustrations. 2nd revised edition. 248pp. 5⅜ x 8. T198 Paperbound **$1.00**

MATHEMAGIC, MAGIC PUZZLES, AND GAMES WITH NUMBERS, R. V. Heath. More than 60 new puzzles and stunts based on the properties of numbers. Easy techniques for multiplying large numbers mentally, revealing hidden numbers magically, finding the date of any day in any year, and dozens more. Over 30 pages devoted to magic squares, triangles, cubes, circles, etc. Edited by J. S. Meyer. 76 illustrations. 128pp. 5⅜ x 8. T110 Paperbound **$1.00**

THE BOOK OF MODERN PUZZLES, G. L. Kaufman. A completely new series of puzzles as fascinating as crossword and deduction puzzles but based upon different principles and techniques. Simple 2-minute teasers, word labyrinths, design and pattern puzzles, logic and observation puzzles — over 150 braincrackers. Answers to all problems. 116 illustrations. 192pp. 5⅜ x 8.
T143 Paperbound **$1.00**

NEW WORD PUZZLES, G. L. Kaufman. 100 ENTIRELY NEW puzzles based on words and their combinations that will delight crossword puzzle, Scrabble and Jotto fans. Chess words, based on the moves of the chess king; design-onyms, symmetrical designs made of synonyms; rhymed double-crostics; syllable sentences; addle letter anagrams; alphagrams; linkograms; and many others all brand new. Full solutions. Space to work problems. 196 figures. vi + 122pp. 5⅜ x 8.
T344 Paperbound **$1.00**

MAZES AND LABYRINTHS: A BOOK OF PUZZLES, W. Shepherd. Mazes, formerly associated with mystery and ritual, are still among the most intriguing of intellectual puzzles. This is a novel and different collection of 50 amusements that embody the principle of the maze: mazes in the classical tradition; 3-dimensional, ribbon, and Möbius-strip mazes; hidden messages; spatial arrangements; etc.—almost all built on amusing story situations. 84 illustrations. Essay on maze psychology. Solutions. xv + 122pp. 5⅜ x 8.
T731 Paperbound **$1.00**

MAGIC TRICKS & CARD TRICKS, W. Jonson. Two books bound as one. 52 tricks with cards, 37 tricks with coins, bills, eggs, smoke, ribbons, slates, etc. Details on presentation, misdirection, and routining will help you master such famous tricks as the Changing Card, Card in the Pocket, Four Aces, Coin Through the Hand, Bill in the Egg, Afghan Bands, and over 75 others. If you follow the lucid exposition and key diagrams carefully, you will finish these two books with an astonishing mastery of magic. 106 figures. 224pp. 5⅜ x 8. T909 Paperbound **$1.00**

PANORAMA OF MAGIC, Milbourne Christopher. A profusely illustrated history of stage magic, a unique selection of prints and engravings from the author's private collection of magic memorabilia, the largest of its kind. Apparatus, stage settings and costumes; ingenious ads distributed by the performers and satiric broadsides passed around in the streets ridiculing pompous showmen; programs; decorative souvenirs. The lively text, by one of America's foremost professional magicians, is full of anecdotes about almost legendary wizards: Dede, the Egyptian; Philadelphia, the wonder-worker; Robert-Houdin, "the father of modern magic;" Harry Houdini; scores more. Altogether a pleasure package for anyone interested in magic, stage setting and design, ethnology, psychology, or simply in unusual people. A Dover original. 295 illustrations; 8 in full color. Index. viii + 216pp. 8⅜ x 11¼.
T774 Paperbound **$2.25**

HOUDINI ON MAGIC, Harry Houdini. One of the greatest magicians of modern times explains his most prized secrets. How locks are picked, with illustrated picks and skeleton keys; how a girl is sawed into twins; how to walk through a brick wall — Houdini's explanations of 44 stage tricks with many diagrams. Also included is a fascinating discussion of great magicians of the past and the story of his fight against fraudulent mediums and spiritualists. Edited by W.B. Gibson and M.N. Young. Bibliography. 155 figures, photos. xv + 280pp. 5⅜ x 8.
T384 Paperbound **$1.35**

MATHEMATICS, MAGIC AND MYSTERY, Martin Gardner. Why do card tricks work? How do magicians perform astonishing mathematical feats? How is stage mind-reading possible? This is the first book length study explaining the application of probability, set theory, theory of numbers, topology, etc., to achieve many startling tricks. Non-technical, accurate, detailed! 115 sections discuss tricks with cards, dice, coins, knots, geometrical vanishing illusions, how a Curry square "demonstrates" that the sum of the parts may be greater than the whole, and dozens of others. No sleight of hand necessary! 135 illustrations. xii + 174pp. 5⅜ x 8.
T335 Paperbound **$1.00**

EASY-TO-DO ENTERTAINMENTS AND DIVERSIONS WITH COINS, CARDS, STRING, PAPER AND MATCHES, R. M. Abraham. Over 300 tricks, games and puzzles will provide young readers with absorbing fun. Sections on card games; paper-folding; tricks with coins, matches and pieces of string; games for the agile; toy-making from common household objects; mathematical recreations; and 50 miscellaneous pastimes. Anyone in charge of groups of youngsters, including hard-pressed parents, and in need of suggestions on how to keep children sensibly amused and quietly content will find this book indispensable. Clear, simple text, copious number of delightful line drawings and illustrative diagrams. Originally titled "Winter Nights Entertainments." Introduction by Lord Baden Powell. 329 illustrations. v + 186pp. 5⅜ x 8½.
T921 Paperbound **$1.00**

STRING FIGURES AND HOW TO MAKE THEM, Caroline Furness Jayne. 107 string figures plus variations selected from the best primitive and modern examples developed by Navajo, Apache, pygmies of Africa, Eskimo, in Europe, Australia, China, etc. The most readily understandable, easy-to-follow book in English on perennially popular recreation. Crystal-clear exposition; step-by-step diagrams. Everyone from kindergarten children to adults looking for unusual diversion will be endlessly amused. Index. Bibliography. Introduction by A. C. Haddon. 17 full-page plates. 960 illustrations. xxiii + 401pp. 5⅜ x 8½.
T152 Paperbound **$2.00**

Entertainments, Humor

ODDITIES AND CURIOSITIES OF WORDS AND LITERATURE, C. Bombaugh, edited by M. Gardner. The largest collection of idiosyncratic prose and poetry techniques in English, a legendary work in the curious and amusing bypaths of literary recreations and the play technique in literature—so important in modern works. Contains alphabetic poetry, acrostics, palindromes, scissors verse, centos, emblematic poetry, famous literary puns, hoaxes, notorious slips of the press, hilarious mistranslations, and much more. Revised and enlarged with modern material by Martin Gardner. 368pp. 5⅜ x 8. T759 Paperbound **$1.50**

A NONSENSE ANTHOLOGY, collected by Carolyn Wells. 245 of the best nonsense verses ever written, including nonsense puns, absurd arguments, mock epics and sagas, nonsense ballads, odes, "sick" verses, dog-Latin verses, French nonsense verses, songs. By Edward Lear, Lewis Carroll, Gelett Burgess, W. S. Gilbert, Hilaire Belloc, Peter Newell, Oliver Herford, etc., 83 writers in all plus over four score anonymous nonsense verses. A special section of limericks, plus famous nonsense such as Carroll's "Jabberwocky" and Lear's "The Jumblies" and much excellent verse virtually impossible to locate elsewhere. For 50 years considered the best anthology available. Index of first lines specially prepared for this edition. Introduction by Carolyn Wells. 3 indexes: Title, Author, First lines. xxxiii + 279pp.
T499 Paperbound **$1.35**

THE BAD CHILD'S BOOK OF BEASTS, MORE BEASTS FOR WORSE CHILDREN, and A MORAL ALPHABET, H. Belloc. Hardly an anthology of humorous verse has appeared in the last 50 years without at least a couple of these famous nonsense verses. But one must see the entire volumes—with all the delightful original illustrations by Sir Basil Blackwood—to appreciate fully Belloc's charming and witty verses that play so subacidly on the platitudes of life and morals that beset his day—and ours. A great humor classic. Three books in one. Total of 157pp. 5⅜ x 8. T749 Paperbound **$1.00**

THE DEVIL'S DICTIONARY, Ambrose Bierce. Sardonic and irreverent barbs puncturing the pomposities and absurdities of American politics, business, religion, literature, and arts, by the country's greatest satirist in the classic tradition. Epigrammatic as Shaw, piercing as Swift, American as Mark Twain, Will Rogers, and Fred Allen, Bierce will always remain the favorite of a small coterie of enthusiasts, and of writers and speakers whom he supplies with "some of the most gorgeous witticisms of the English language" (H. L. Mencken). Over 1000 entries in alphabetical order. 144pp. 5⅜ x 8. T487 Paperbound **$1.00**

THE PURPLE COW AND OTHER NONSENSE, Gelett Burgess. The best of Burgess's early nonsense, selected from the first edition of the "Burgess Nonsense Book." Contains many of his most unusual and truly awe-inspiring pieces: 36 nonsense quatrains, the Poems of Patagonia, Alphabet of Famous Goops, and the other hilarious (and rare) adult nonsense that place him in the forefront of American humorists. All pieces are accompanied by the original Burgess illustrations. 123 illustrations. xiii + 113pp. 5⅜ x 8. T772 Paperbound **$1.00**

MY PIOUS FRIENDS AND DRUNKEN COMPANIONS and MORE PIOUS FRIENDS AND DRUNKEN COMPANIONS, Frank Shay. Folksingers, amateur and professional, and everyone who loves singing: here, available for the first time in 30 years, is this valued collection of 132 ballads, blues, vaudeville numbers, drinking songs, sea chanties, comedy songs. Songs of pre-Beatnik Bohemia; songs from all over America, England, France, Australia; the great songs of the Naughty Nineties and early twentieth-century America. Over a third with music. Woodcuts by John Held, Jr. convey perfectly the brash insouciance of an era of rollicking unabashed song. 12 illustrations by John Held, Jr. Two indexes (Titles and First lines and Choruses). Introductions by the author. Two volumes bound as one. Total of xvi + 235pp. 5⅜ x 8½.
T946 Paperbound **$1.25**

HOW TO TELL THE BIRDS FROM THE FLOWERS, R. W. Wood. How not to confuse a carrot with a parrot, a grape with an ape, a puffin with nuffin. Delightful drawings, clever puns, absurd little poems point out far-fetched resemblances in nature. The author was a leading physicist. Introduction by Margaret Wood White. 106 illus. 60pp. 5⅜ x 8.
T523 Paperbound **75¢**

PECK'S BAD BOY AND HIS PA, George W. Peck. The complete edition, containing both volumes, of one of the most widely read American humor books. The endless ingenious pranks played by bad boy "Hennery" on his pa and the grocery man, the outraged pomposity of Pa, the perpetual ridiculing of middle class institutions, are as entertaining today as they were in 1883. No pale sophistications or subtleties, but rather humor vigorous, raw, earthy, imaginative, and, as folk humor often is, sadistic. This peculiarly fascinating book is also valuable to historians and students of American culture as a portrait of an age. 100 original illustrations by True Williams. Introduction by E. F. Bleiler. 347pp. 5⅜ x 8.
T497 Paperbound **$1.35**

THE HUMOROUS VERSE OF LEWIS CARROLL. Almost every poem Carroll ever wrote, the largest collection ever published, including much never published elsewhere: 150 parodies, burlesques, riddles, ballads, acrostics, etc., with 130 original illustrations by Tenniel, Carroll, and others. "Addicts will be grateful . . . there is nothing for the faithful to do but sit down and fall to the banquet," N. Y. Times. Index to first lines. xiv + 446pp. 5⅜ x 8.
T654 Paperbound **$2.00**

DIVERSIONS AND DIGRESSIONS OF LEWIS CARROLL. A major new treasure for Carroll fans! Rare privately published humor, fantasy, puzzles, and games by Carroll at his whimsical best, with a new vein of frank satire. Includes many new mathematical amusements and recreations, among them the fragmentary Part III of "Curiosa Mathematica." Contains "The Rectory Umbrella," "The New Belfry," "The Vision of the Three T's," and much more. New 32-page supplement of rare photographs taken by Carroll. x + 375pp. 5⅜ x 8.
T732 Paperbound **$1.65**

THE COMPLETE NONSENSE OF EDWARD LEAR. This is the only complete edition of this master of gentle madness available at a popular price. A BOOK OF NONSENSE, NONSENSE SONGS, MORE NONSENSE SONGS AND STORIES in their entirety with all the old favorites that have delighted children and adults for years. The Dong With A Luminous Nose, The Jumblies, The Owl and the Pussycat, and hundreds of other bits of wonderful nonsense. 214 limericks, 3 sets of Nonsense Botany, 5 Nonsense Alphabets, 546 drawings by Lear himself, and much more. 320pp. 5⅜ x 8.
T167 Paperbound **$1.00**

THE MELANCHOLY LUTE, The Humorous Verse of Franklin P. Adams ("FPA"). The author's own selection of light verse, drawn from thirty years of FPA's column, "The Conning Tower," syndicated all over the English-speaking world. Witty, perceptive, literate, these ninety-six poems range from parodies of other poets, Millay, Longfellow, Edgar Guest, Kipling, Masefield, etc., and free and hilarious translations of Horace and other Latin poets, to satiric comments on fabled American institutions—the New York Subways, preposterous ads, suburbanites, sensational journalism, etc. They reveal with vigor and clarity the humor, integrity and restraint of a wise and gentle American satirist. Introduction by Robert Hutchinson. vi + 122pp. 5⅜ x 8½.
T108 Paperbound **$1.00**

SINGULAR TRAVELS, CAMPAIGNS, AND ADVENTURES OF BARON MUNCHAUSEN, R. E. Raspe, with 90 illustrations by Gustave Doré. The first edition in over 150 years to reestablish the deeds of the Prince of Liars exactly as Raspe first recorded them in 1785—the genuine Baron Munchausen, one of the most popular personalities in English literature. Included also are the best of the many sequels, written by other hands. Introduction on Raspe by J. Carswell. Bibliography of early editions. xliv + 192pp. 5⅜ x 8.
T698 Paperbound **$1.00**

THE WIT AND HUMOR OF OSCAR WILDE, ed. by Alvin Redman. Wilde at his most brilliant, in 1000 epigrams exposing weaknesses and hypocrisies of "civilized" society. Divided into 49 categories—sin, wealth, women, America, etc.—to aid writers, speakers. Includes excerpts from his trials, books, plays, criticism. Formerly "The Epigrams of Oscar Wilde." Introduction by Vyvyan Holland, Wilde's only living son. Introductory essay by editor. 260pp. 5⅜ x 8.
T602 Paperbound **$1.00**

MAX AND MORITZ, Wilhelm Busch. Busch is one of the great humorists of all time, as well as the father of the modern comic strip. This volume, translated by H. A. Klein and other hands, contains the perennial favorite "Max and Moritz" (translated by C. T. Brooks), Plisch and Plum, Das Rabennest, Eispeter, and seven other whimsical, sardonic, jovial, diabolical cartoon and verse stories. Lively English translations parallel the original German. This work has delighted millions, since it first appeared in the 19th century, and is guaranteed to please almost anyone. Edited by H. A. Klein, with an afterword. x + 205pp. 5⅝ x 8½.
T181 Paperbound **$1.15**

HYPOCRITICAL HELENA, Wilhelm Busch. A companion volume to "Max and Moritz," with the title piece (Die Fromme Helena) and 10 other highly amusing cartoon and verse stories, all newly translated by H. A. Klein and M. C. Klein: Adventure on New Year's Eve (Abenteuer in der Neujahrsnacht), Hangover on the Morning after New Year's Eve (Der Katzenjammer am Neujahrsmorgen), etc. English and German in parallel columns. Hours of pleasure, also a fine language aid. x + 205pp. 5⅝ x 8½.
T184 Paperbound **$1.00**

THE BEAR THAT WASN'T, Frank Tashlin. What does it mean? Is it simply delightful wry humor, or a charming story of a bear who wakes up in the midst of a factory, or a satire on Big Business, or an existential cartoon-story of the human condition, or a symbolization of the struggle between conformity and the individual? New York Herald Tribune said of the first edition: ". . . a fable for grownups that will be fun for children. Sit down with the book and get your own bearings." Long an underground favorite with readers of all ages and opinions. v + 51pp. Illustrated. 5⅜ x 8½.
T939 Paperbound **75¢**

RUTHLESS RHYMES FOR HEARTLESS HOMES and MORE RUTHLESS RHYMES FOR HEARTLESS HOMES, Harry Graham ("Col. D. Streamer"). Two volumes of Little Willy and 48 other poetic disasters. A bright, new reprint of oft-quoted, never forgotten, devastating humor by a precursor of today's "sick" joke school. For connoisseurs of wicked, wacky humor and all who delight in the comedy of manners. Original drawings are a perfect complement. 61 illustrations. Index. vi + 69pp. Two vols. bound as one. 5⅜ x 8½.
T930 Paperbound **75¢**

Say It language phrase books

These handy phrase books (128 to 196 pages each) make grammatical drills unnecessary for an elementary knowledge of a spoken foreign language. Covering most matters of travel and everyday life each volume contains:

Over 1000 phrases and sentences in immediately useful forms — foreign language plus English.

Modern usage designed for Americans. Specific phrases like, "Give me small change," and "Please call a taxi."

Simplified phonetic transcription you will be able to read at sight.

The only completely indexed phrase books on the market.

Covers scores of important situations: — Greetings, restaurants, sightseeing, useful expressions, etc.

These books are prepared by native linguists who are professors at Columbia, N.Y.U., Fordham and other great universities. Use them independently or with any other book or record course. They provide a supplementary living element that most other courses lack. Individual volumes in:

Russian 75¢	Italian 75¢	Spanish 75¢	German 75¢
Hebrew 75¢	Danish 75¢	Japanese 75¢	Swedish 75¢
Dutch 75¢	Esperanto 75¢	Modern Greek 75¢	Portuguese 75¢
Norwegian 75¢	Polish 75¢	French 75¢	Yiddish 75¢
Turkish 75¢		English for German-speaking people 75¢	
English for Italian-speaking people 75¢		English for Spanish-speaking people 75¢	

Large clear type. 128-196 pages each. 3½ x 5¼. Sturdy paper binding.

Listen and Learn language records

LISTEN & LEARN is the only language record course designed especially to meet your travel and everyday needs. It is available in separate sets for FRENCH, SPANISH, GERMAN, JAPANESE, RUSSIAN, MODERN GREEK, PORTUGUESE, ITALIAN and HEBREW, and each set contains three 33⅓ rpm long-playing records—1½ hours of recorded speech by eminent native speakers who are professors at Columbia, New York University, Queens College.

Check the following special features found only in LISTEN & LEARN:

- **Dual-language recording.** 812 selected phrases and sentences, over 3200 words, spoken first in English, then in their foreign language equivalents. A suitable pause follows each foreign phrase, allowing you time to repeat the expression. You learn by unconscious assimilation.

- **128 to 206-page manual** contains everything on the records, plus a simple phonetic pronunciation guide.

- **Indexed for convenience. The only set on the market** that is completely indexed. No more puzzling over where to find the phrase you need. Just look in the rear of the manual.

- **Practical.** No time wasted on material you can find in any grammar. LISTEN & LEARN covers central core material with phrase approach. Ideal for the person with limited learning time.

- **Living, modern expressions,** not found in other courses. Hygienic products, modern equipment, shopping—expressions used every day, like "nylon" and "air-conditioned."

- **Limited objective.** Everything you learn, no matter where you stop, is immediately useful. You have to finish other courses, wade through grammar and vocabulary drill, before they help you.

- **High-fidelity recording.** LISTEN & LEARN records equal in clarity and surface-silence any record on the market costing up to $6.

"Excellent . . . the spoken records . . . impress me as being among the very best on the market," **Prof. Mario Pei,** Dept. of Romance Languages, Columbia University. "Inexpensive and well-done . . . it would make an ideal present," CHICAGO SUNDAY TRIBUNE. "More genuinely helpful than anything of its kind which I have previously encountered," **Sidney Clark,** well-known author of "ALL THE BEST" travel books.

UNCONDITIONAL GUARANTEE. Try LISTEN & LEARN, then return it within 10 days for full refund if you are not satisfied.

Each set contains three twelve-inch 33⅓ records, manual, and album.

SPANISH	the set $5.95	GERMAN	the set $5.95
FRENCH	the set $5.95	ITALIAN	the set $5.95
RUSSIAN	the set $5.95	JAPANESE	the set $5.95
PORTUGUESE	the set $5.95	MODERN GREEK	the set $5.95
MODERN HEBREW	the set $5.95		

Americana

THE EYES OF DISCOVERY, J. Bakeless. A vivid reconstruction of how unspoiled America appeared to the first white men. Authentic and enlightening accounts of Hudson's landing in New York, Coronado's trek through the Southwest; scores of explorers, settlers, trappers, soldiers. America's pristine flora, fauna, and Indians in every region and state in fresh and unusual new aspects. "A fascinating view of what the land was like before the first highway went through," Time. 68 contemporary illustrations, 39 newly added in this edition. Index. Bibliography. x + 500pp. 5⅜ x 8.　　　　　　　　　　　　　　　**T761 Paperbound $2.00**

AUDUBON AND HIS JOURNALS, J. J. Audubon. A collection of fascinating accounts of Europe and America in the early 1800's through Audubon's own eyes. Includes the Missouri River Journals —an eventful trip through America's untouched heartland, the Labrador Journals, the European Journals, the famous "Episodes", and other rare Audubon material, including the descriptive chapters from the original letterpress edition of the "Ornithological Studies", omitted in all later editions. Indispensable for ornithologists, naturalists, and all lovers of Americana and adventure. 70-page biography by Audubon's granddaughter. 38 illustrations. Total of 1106pp. 5⅜ x 8.

　　　　　　　　　　　　　　　　　　　　　　　　　　T675 Vol I Paperbound $2.25
　　　　　　　　　　　　　　　　　　　　　　　　　　T676 Vol II Paperbound $2.25
　　　　　　　　　　　　　　　　　　　　　　　　　　　　　　　　　The set $4.50

TRAVELS OF WILLIAM BARTRAM, edited by Mark Van Doren. The first inexpensive illustrated edition of one of the 18th century's most delightful books is an excellent source of first-hand material on American geography, anthropology, and natural history. Many descriptions of early Indian tribes are our only source of information on them prior to the infiltration of the white man. "The mind of a scientist with the soul of a poet," John Livingston Lowes. 13 original illustrations and maps. Edited with an introduction by Mark Van Doren. 448pp. 5⅜ x 8.
　　　　　　　　　　　　　　　　　　　　　　　　　　　　　　T13 Paperbound $2.00

GARRETS AND PRETENDERS: A HISTORY OF BOHEMIANISM IN AMERICA, A. Parry. The colorful and fantastic history of American Bohemianism from Poe to Kerouac. This is the only complete record of hoboes, cranks, starving poets, and suicides. Here are Pfaff, Whitman, Crane, Bierce, Pound, and many others. New chapters by the author and by H. T. Moore bring this thorough and well-documented history down to the Beatniks. "An excellent account," N. Y. Times. Scores of cartoons, drawings, and caricatures. Bibliography. Index. xxviii + 421pp. 5⅝ x 8⅜.　　　　　　　　　　　　　　　　　　　　**T708 Paperbound $1.95**

THE EXPLORATION OF THE COLORADO RIVER AND ITS CANYONS, J. W. Powell. The thrilling first-hand account of the expedition that filled in the last white space on the map of the United States. Rapids, famine, hostile Indians, and mutiny are among the perils encountered as the unknown Colorado Valley reveals its secrets. This is the only uncut version of Major Powell's classic of exploration that has been printed in the last 60 years. Includes later reflections and subsequent expedition. 250 illustrations, new map. 400pp. 5⅝ x 8⅜.
　　　　　　　　　　　　　　　　　　　　　　　　　　　　　　T94 Paperbound $2.25

THE JOURNAL OF HENRY D. THOREAU, Edited by Bradford Torrey and Francis H. Allen. Henry Thoreau is not only one of the most important figures in American literature and social thought; his voluminous journals (from which his books emerged as selections and crystalliza-tions) constitute both the longest, most sensitive record of personal internal development and a most penetrating description of a historical moment in American culture. This present set, which was first issued in fourteen volumes, contains Thoreau's entire journals from 1837 to 1862, with the exception of the lost years which were found only recently. We are reissuing it, complete and unabridged, with a new introduction by Walter Harding, Secretary of the Thoreau Society. Fourteen volumes reissued in two volumes. Foreword by Henry Seidel Canby. Total of 1888pp. 8⅜ x 12¼.　　　　　**T312-3 Two volume set, Clothbound $20.00**

GAMES AND SONGS OF AMERICAN CHILDREN, collected by William Wells Newell. A remarkable collection of 190 games with songs that accompany many of them; cross references to show similarities, differences among them; variations; musical notation for 38 songs. Textual dis-cussions show relations with folk-drama and other aspects of folk tradition. Grouped into categories for ready comparative study: Love-games, histories, playing at work, human life, bird and beast, mythology, guessing-games, etc. New introduction covers relations of songs and dances to timeless heritage of folklore, biographical sketch of Newell, other pertinent data. A good source of inspiration for those in charge of groups of children and a valuable reference for anthropologists, sociologists, psychiatrists. Introduction by Carl Withers. New indexes of first lines, games. 5⅜ x 8½. xii + 242pp.　　　　　　**T354 Paperbound $1.75**

Art, History of Art, Antiques, Graphic Arts, Handcrafts

ART STUDENTS' ANATOMY, E. J. Farris. Outstanding art anatomy that uses chiefly living objects for its illustrations. 71 photos of undraped men, women, children are accompanied by carefully labeled matching sketches to illustrate the skeletal system, articulations and movements, bony landmarks, the muscular system, skin, fasciae, fat, etc. 9 x-ray photos show movement of joints. Undraped models are shown in such actions as serving in tennis, drawing a bow in archery, playing football, dancing, preparing to spring and to dive. Also discussed and illustrated are proportions, age and sex differences, the anatomy of the smile, etc. 8 plates by the great early 18th century anatomic illustrator Siegfried Albinus are also included. Glossary. 158 figures, 7 in color. x + 159pp. 5⅝ x 8⅜.   T744 Paperbound **$1.50**

AN ATLAS OF ANATOMY FOR ARTISTS, F Schider. A new 3rd edition of this standard text enlarged by 52 new illustrations of hands, anatomical studies by Cloquet, and expressive life studies of the body by Barcsay. 189 clear, detailed plates offer you precise information of impeccable accuracy. 29 plates show all aspects of the skeleton, with closeups of special areas, while 54 full-page plates, mostly in two colors, give human musculature as seen from four different points of view, with cutaways for important portions of the body. 14 full-page plates provide photographs of hand forms, eyelids, female breasts, and indicate the location of muscles upon models. 59 additional plates show how great artists of the past utilized human anatomy. They reproduce sketches and finished work by such artists as Michelangelo, Leonardo da Vinci, Goya, and 15 others. This is a lifetime reference work which will be one of the most important books in any artist's library. "The standard reference tool," AMERICAN LIBRARY ASSOCIATION. "Excellent," AMERICAN ARTIST. Third enlarged edition. 189 plates, 647 illustrations. xxvi + 192pp. 7⅞ x 10⅝.   T241 Clothbound **$6.00**

AN ATLAS OF ANIMAL ANATOMY FOR ARTISTS, W. Ellenberger, H. Baum, H. Dittrich. The largest, richest animal anatomy for artists available in English. 99 detailed anatomical plates of such animals as the horse, dog, cat, lion, deer, seal, kangaroo, flying squirrel, cow, bull, goat, monkey, hare, and bat. Surface features are clearly indicated, while progressive beneath-the-skin pictures show musculature, tendons, and bone structure. Rest and action are exhibited in terms of musculature and skeletal structure and detailed cross-sections are given for heads and important features. The animals chosen are representative of specific families so that a study of these anatomies will provide knowledge of hundreds of related species. "Highly recommended as one of the very few books on the subject worthy of being used as an authoritative guide," DESIGN. "Gives a fundamental knowledge," AMERICAN ARTIST. Second revised, enlarged edition with new plates from Cuvier, Stubbs, etc. 288 illustrations. 153pp. 11⅜ x 9.   T82 Clothbound **$6.00**

THE HUMAN FIGURE IN MOTION, Eadweard Muybridge. The largest selection in print of Muybridge's famous high-speed action photos of the human figure in motion. 4789 photographs illustrate 162 different actions: men, women, children—mostly undraped—are shown walking, running, carrying various objects, sitting, lying down, climbing, throwing, arising, and performing over 150 other actions. Some actions are shown in as many as 150 photographs each. All in all there are more than 500 action strips in this enormous volume, series shots taken at shutter speeds of as high as 1/6000th of a second! These are not posed shots, but true stopped motion. They show bone and muscle in situations that the human eye is not fast enough to capture. Earlier, smaller editions of these prints have brought $40 and more on the out-of-print market. "A must for artists," ART IN FOCUS. "An unparalleled dictionary of action for all artists," AMERICAN ARTIST. 390 full-page plates, with 4789 photographs. Printed on heavy glossy stock. Reinforced binding with headbands. xxi + 390pp. 7⅞ x 10⅝.
T204 Clothbound **$10.00**

ANIMALS IN MOTION, Eadweard Muybridge. This is the largest collection of animal action photos in print. 34 different animals (horses, mules, oxen, goats, camels, pigs, cats, guanacos, lions, gnus, deer, monkeys, eagles—and 21 others) in 132 characteristic actions. The horse alone is shown in more than 40 different actions. All 3919 photographs are taken in series at speeds up to 1/6000th of a second. The secrets of leg motion, spinal patterns, head movements, strains and contortions shown nowhere else are captured. You will see exactly how a lion sets his foot down; how an elephant's knees are like a human's—and how they differ; the position of a kangaroo's legs in mid-leap; how an ostrich's head bobs; details of the flight of birds—and thousands of facets of motion only the fastest cameras can catch. Photographed from domestic animals and animals in the Philadelphia zoo, it contains neither semiposed artificial shots nor distorted telephoto shots taken under adverse conditions. Artists, biologists, decorators, cartoonists, will find this book indispensable for understanding animals in motion. "A really marvelous series of plates," NATURE (London). "The dry plate's most spectacular early use was by Eadweard Muybridge," LIFE. 3919 photographs; 380 full pages of plates. 440pp. Printed on heavy glossy paper. Deluxe binding with headbands. 7⅞ x 10⅝.
T203 Clothbound **$10.00**

CATALOGUE OF DOVER BOOKS

THE AUTOBIOGRAPHY OF AN IDEA, Louis Sullivan. The pioneer architect whom Frank Lloyd Wright called "the master" reveals an acute sensitivity to social forces and values in this passionately honest account. He records the crystallization of his opinions and theories, the growth of his organic theory of architecture that still influences American designers and architects, contemporary ideas, etc. This volume contains the first appearance of 34 full-page plates of his finest architecture. Unabridged reissue of 1924 edition. New introduction by R. M. Line. Index. xiv + 335pp. 5⅜ x 8. T281 Paperbound **$2.00**

THE DRAWINGS OF HEINRICH KLEY. The first uncut republication of both of Kley's devastating sketchbooks, which first appeared in pre-World War I Germany. One of the greatest cartoonists and social satirists of modern times, his exuberant and iconoclastic fantasy and his extraordinary technique place him in the great tradition of Bosch, Breughel, and Goya, while his subject matter has all the immediacy and tension of our century. 200 drawings. viii + 128pp. 7¾ x 10¾. T24 Paperbound **$1.85**

MORE DRAWINGS BY HEINRICH KLEY. All the sketches from Leut' Und Viecher (1912) and Sammel-Album (1923) not included in the previous Dover edition of Drawings. More of the bizarre, mercilessly iconoclastic sketches that shocked and amused on their original publication. Nothing was too sacred, no one too eminent for satirization by this imaginative, individual and accomplished master cartoonist. A total of 158 illustrations. Iv + 104pp. 7¾ x 10¾. T41 Paperbound **$1.85**

PINE FURNITURE OF EARLY NEW ENGLAND, R. H. Kettell. A rich understanding of one of America's most original folk arts that collectors of antiques, interior decorators, craftsmen, woodworkers, and everyone interested in American history and art will find fascinating and immensely useful. 413 illustrations of more than 300 chairs, benches, racks, beds, cupboards, mirrors, shelves, tables, and other furniture will show all the simple beauty and character of early New England furniture. 55 detailed drawings carefully analyze outstanding pieces. "With its rich store of illustrations, this book emphasizes the individuality and varied design of early American pine furniture. It should be welcomed," ANTIQUES. 413 illustrations and 55 working drawings. 475. 8 x 10¾. T145 Clothbound **$10.00**

THE HUMAN FIGURE, J. H. Vanderpoel. Every important artistic element of the human figure is pointed out in minutely detailed word descriptions in this classic text and illustrated as well in 430 pencil and charcoal drawings. Thus the text of this book directs your attention to all the characteristic features and subtle differences of the male and female (adults, children, and aged persons), as though a master artist were telling you what to look for at each stage. 2nd edition, revised and enlarged by George Bridgman. Foreword. 430 illustrations. 143pp. 6⅛ x 9¼. T432 Paperbound **$1.50**

LETTERING AND ALPHABETS, J. A. Cavanagh. This unabridged reissue of LETTERING offers a full discussion, analysis, illustration of 89 basic hand lettering styles — styles derived from Caslons, Bodonis, Garamonds, Gothic, Black Letter, Oriental, and many others. Upper and lower cases, numerals and common signs pictured. Hundreds of technical hints on make-up, construction, artistic validity, strokes, pens, brushes, white areas, etc. May be reproduced without permission! 89 complete alphabets; 72 lettered specimens. 121pp. 9¾ x 8. T53 Paperbound **$1.35**

STICKS AND STONES, Lewis Mumford. A survey of the forces that have conditioned American architecture and altered its forms. The author discusses the medieval tradition in early New England villages; the Renaissance influence which developed with the rise of the merchant class; the classical influence of Jefferson's time; the "Mechanicsvilles" of Poe's generation; the Brown Decades; the philosophy of the Imperial facade; and finally the modern machine age. "A truly remarkable book," SAT. REV. OF LITERATURE. 2nd revised edition. 21 illustrations. xvii + 228pp. 5⅜ x 8. T202 Paperbound **$1.65**

THE STANDARD BOOK OF QUILT MAKING AND COLLECTING, Marguerite Ickis. A complete easy-to-follow guide with all the information you need to make beautiful, useful quilts. How to plan, design, cut, sew, appliqué, avoid sewing problems, use rag bag, make borders, tuft, every other aspect. Over 100 traditional quilts shown, including over 40 full-size patterns. At-home hobby for fun, profit. Index. 483 illus. 1 color plate. 287pp. 6¾ x 9½. T582 Paperbound **$2.00**

THE BOOK OF SIGNS, Rudolf Koch. Formerly $20 to $25 on the out-of-print market, now only $1.00 in this unabridged new edition! 493 symbols from ancient manuscripts, medieval cathedrals, coins, catacombs, pottery, etc. Crosses, monograms of Roman emperors, astrological, chemical, botanical, runes, housemarks, and 7 other categories. Invaluable for handicraft workers, illustrators, scholars, etc., this material may be reproduced without permission. 493 illustrations by Fritz Kredel. 104pp. 6½ x 9¼. T162 Paperbound **$1.00**

PRIMITIVE ART, Franz Boas. This authoritative and exhaustive work by a great American anthropologist covers the entire gamut of primitive art. Pottery, leatherwork, metal work, stone work, wood, basketry, are treated in detail. Theories of primitive art, historical depth in art history, technical virtuosity, unconscious levels of patterning, symbolism, styles, literature, music, dance, etc. A must book for the interested layman, the anthropologist, artist, handicrafter (hundreds of unusual motifs), and the historian. Over 900 illustrations (50 ceramic vessels, 12 totem poles, etc.). 376pp. 5⅜ x 8. T25 Paperbound **$2.00**

Fiction

THE LAND THAT TIME FORGOT and THE MOON MAID, Edgar Rice Burroughs. In the opinion of many, Burroughs' best work. The first concerns a strange island where evolution is individual rather than phylogenetic. Speechless anthropoids develop into intelligent human beings within a single generation. The second projects the reader far into the future and describes the first voyage to the Moon (in the year 2025), the conquest of the Earth by the Moon, and years of violence and adventure as the enslaved Earthmen try to regain possession of their planet. "An imaginative tour de force that keeps the reader keyed up and expectant," NEW YORK TIMES. Complete, unabridged text of the original two novels (three parts in each). 5 illustrations by J. Allen St. John. vi + 552pp. 5⅜ x 8½.
T1020 Clothbound **$3.75**
T358 Paperbound **$2.00**

AT THE EARTH'S CORE, PELLUCIDAR, TANAR OF PELLUCIDAR: THREE SCIENCE FICTION NOVELS BY EDGAR RICE BURROUGHS. Complete, unabridged texts of the first three Pellucidar novels. Tales of derring-do by the famous master of science fiction. The locale for these three related stories is the inner surface of the hollow Earth where we discover the world of Pellucidar, complete with all types of bizarre, menacing creatures, strange peoples, and alluring maidens—guaranteed to delight all Burroughs fans and a wide circle of adventure lovers. Illustrated by J. Allen St. John and P. F. Berdanier. vi + 433pp. 5⅜ x 8½.
T1051 Paperbound **$2.00**

THREE MARTIAN NOVELS, Edgar Rice Burroughs. Contains: Thuvia, Maid of Mars; The Chessmen of Mars; and The Master Mind of Mars. High adventure set in an imaginative and intricate conception of the Red Planet. Mars is peopled with an intelligent, heroic human race which lives in densely populated cities and with fierce barbarians who inhabit dead sea bottoms. Other exciting creatures abound amidst an inventive framework of Martian history and geography. Complete unabridged reprintings of the first edition. 16 illustrations by J. Allen St. John. vi + 499pp. 5⅜ x 8½.
T39 Paperbound **$1.85**

TO THE SUN? and OFF ON A COMET!, Jules Verne. Complete texts of two of the most imaginative flights into fancy in world literature display the high adventure that have kept Verne's novels read for nearly a century. Only unabridged edition of the best translation, by Edward Roth. Large, easily readable type. 50 illustrations selected from first editions. 462pp. 5⅜ x 8.
T634 Paperbound **$1.75**

FROM THE EARTH TO THE MOON and ALL AROUND THE MOON, Jules Verne. Complete editions of two of Verne's most successful novels, in finest Edward Roth translations, now available after many years out of print. Verne's visions of submarines, airplanes, television, rockets, interplanetary travel; of scientific and not-so-scientific beliefs; of peculiarities of Americans; all delight and engross us today as much as when they first appeared. Large, easily readable type. 42 illus. from first French edition. 476pp. 5⅜ x 8.
T633 Paperbound **$1.75**

THREE PROPHETIC NOVELS BY H. G. WELLS, edited by E. F. Bleiler. Complete texts of "When the Sleeper Wakes" (1st book printing in 50 years), "A Story of the Days to Come," "The Time Machine" (1st complete printing in book form). Exciting adventures in the future are as enjoyable today as 50 years ago when first printed. Predict TV, movies, intercontinental airplanes, prefabricated houses, air-conditioned cities, etc. First important author to foresee problems of mind control, technological dictatorships. "Absolute best of imaginative fiction," N. Y. Times. Introduction. 335pp. 5⅜ x 8.
T605 Paperbound **$1.50**

SEVEN SCIENCE FICTION NOVELS, H. G. Wells. Full unabridged texts of 7 science-fiction novels of the master. Ranging from biology, physics, chemistry, astronomy to sociology and other studies, Mr. Wells extrapolates whole worlds of strange and intriguing character. "One will have to go far to match this for entertainment, excitement, and sheer pleasure . . . ," NEW YORK TIMES. Contents: The Time Machine, The Island of Dr. Moreau, First Men in the Moon, The Invisible Man, The War of the Worlds, The Food of the Gods, In the Days of the Comet. 1015pp. 5⅜ x 8.
T264 Clothbound **$4.50**

28 SCIENCE FICTION STORIES OF H. G. WELLS. Two full unabridged novels, MEN LIKE GODS and STAR BEGOTTEN, plus 26 short stories by the master science-fiction writer of all time. Stories of space, time, invention, exploration, future adventure—an indispensable part of the library of everyone interested in science and adventure. PARTIAL CONTENTS: Men Like Gods, The Country of the Blind, In the Abyss, The Crystal Egg, The Man Who Could Work Miracles, A Story of the Days to Come, The Valley of Spiders, and 21 more! 928pp. 5⅜ x 8.
T265 Clothbound **$4.50**

THE WAR IN THE AIR, IN THE DAYS OF THE COMET, THE FOOD OF THE GODS: THREE SCIENCE FICTION NOVELS BY H. G. WELLS. Three exciting Wells offerings bearing on vital social and philosophical issues of his and our own day. Here are tales of air power, strategic bombing, East vs. West, the potential miracles of science, the potential disasters from outer space, the relationship between scientific advancement and moral progress, etc. First reprinting of "War in the Air" in almost 50 years. An excellent sampling of Wells at his storytelling best. Complete, unabridged reprintings. 16 illustrations. 645pp. 5⅜ x 8½.
T1135 Paperbound **$2.00**

Music

A GENERAL HISTORY OF MUSIC, Charles Burney. A detailed coverage of music from the Greeks up to 1789, with full information on all types of music: sacred and secular, vocal and instrumental, operatic and symphonic. Theory, notation, forms, instruments, innovators, composers, performers, typical and important works, and much more in an easy, entertaining style. Burney covered much of Europe and spoke with hundreds of authorities and composers so that this work is more than a compilation of records . . . it is a living work of careful and first-hand scholarship. Its account of thoroughbass (18th century) Italian music is probably still the best introduction on the subject. A recent NEW YORK TIMES review said, "Surprisingly few of Burney's statements have been invalidated by modern research . . . still of great value." Edited and corrected by Frank Mercer. 35 figures. Indices. 1915pp. 5⅜ x 8. 2 volumes. **T36 The Set, Clothbound $12.50**

A DICTIONARY OF HYMNOLOGY, John Julian. This exhaustive and scholarly work has become known as an invaluable source of hundreds of thousands of important and often difficult to obtain facts on the history and use of hymns in the western world. Everyone interested in hymns will be fascinated by the accounts of famous hymns and hymn writers and amazed by the amount of practical information he will find. More than 30,000 entries on individual hymns, giving authorship, date and circumstances of composition, publication, textual variations, translations, denominational and ritual usage, etc. Biographies of more than 9,000 hymn writers, and essays on important topics such as Christmas carols and children's hymns, and much other unusual and valuable information. A 200 page double-columned index of first lines — the largest in print. Total of 1786 pages in two reinforced clothbound volumes. 6¼ x 9¼. **The set, T333 Clothbound $17.50**

MUSIC IN MEDIEVAL BRITAIN, F. Ll. Harrison. The most thorough, up-to-date, and accurate treatment of the subject ever published, beautifully illustrated. Complete account of institutions and choirs; carols, masses, and motets; liturgy and plainsong; and polyphonic music from the Norman Conquest to the Reformation. Discusses the various schools of music and their reciprocal influences; the origin and development of new ritual forms; development and use of instruments; and new evidence on many problems of the period. Reproductions of scores, over 200 excerpts from medieval melodies. Rules of harmony and dissonance; influence of Continental styles; great composers (Dunstable, Cornysh, Fairfax, etc.); and much more. Register and index of more than 400 musicians. Index of titles. General Index. 225-item bibliography. 6 Appendices. xix + 491pp. 5⅝ x 8¾. **T705 Clothbound $10.00**

THE MUSIC OF SPAIN, Gilbert Chase. Only book in English to give concise, comprehensive account of Iberian music; new Chapter covers music since 1941. Victoria, Albéniz, Cabezón, Pedrell, Turina, hundreds of other composers; popular and folk music; the Gypsies; the guitar; dance, theatre, opera, with only extensive discussion in English of the Zarzuela; virtuosi such as Casals; much more. "Distinguished . . . readable," Saturday Review. 400-item bibliography. Index. 27 photos. 383pp. 5⅜ x 8. **T549 Paperbound $2.00**

ON STUDYING SINGING, Sergius Kagen. An intelligent method of voice-training, which leads you around pitfalls that waste your time, money, and effort. Exposes rigid, mechanical systems, baseless theories, deleterious exercises. "Logical, clear, convincing . . . dead right," Virgil Thomson, N.Y. Herald Tribune. "I recommend this volume highly," Maggie Teyte, Saturday Review. 119pp. 5⅜ x 8. **T622 Paperbound $1.25**

Prices subject to change without notice.

Dover publishes books on art, music, philosophy, literature, languages, history, social sciences, psychology, handcrafts, orientalia, puzzles and entertainments, chess, pets and gardens, books explaining science, intermediate and higher mathematics, mathematical physics, engineering, biological sciences, earth sciences, classics of science, etc. Write to:

Dept. catrr.
Dover Publications, Inc.
180 Varick Street, N.Y. 14, N.Y.